Climate Change Management

Climate Change Management

Special Topics in the Context of Asia

Edited by

Huong Ha

BEP BUSINESS EXPERT PRESS

Climate Change Management: Special Topics in the Context of Asia

First published in 2018 by
Business Expert Press, LLC
222 East 46th Street, New York, NY 10017
www.businessexpertpress.com

ISBN-13: 978-1-94784-327-1 (paperback)
ISBN-13: 978-1-94784-328-8 (e-book)

Business Expert Press Environmental and Social Sustainability for Business Advantage Collection

Collection ISSN: 2327-333X (print)
Collection ISSN: 2327-3348 (electronic)

Cover and interior design by Exeter Premedia Services Private Ltd., Chennai, India

First edition: 2018

10 9 8 7 6 5 4 3 2 1

Printed in the United States of America.

Abstract

This book includes seven chapters focusing on special issues of climate change management in Asia. The first chapter discusses the challenges with regard to climate change governance. The second chapter examines the impact of climate change on agriculture and food security in Nepal from socio-economic perspectives. The findings reveal that climate change entails much adverse effect, for example, contributing to loss of species and local landraces, reducing agricultural productivity and yield, and contributing to the emerged labor crisis in the rural areas. The third chapter is a rare work which explores a new dimension of climate change management, that is, environmental knowledge management. The fourth chapter also touches on a special topic regarding climate change, that is, legal issues in the maritime sector. This chapter reviews the climate change challenges faced by the maritime industry, and the current legal framework governing the maritime sector in South Asia with regard to climate change. The fifth chapter examines how the legal industry in Malaysia responds to climate change to contribute to resolving such global issues, and to the development of the country's economic growth. The sixth chapter, about the agriculture sector in Japan, investigates whether the adaptive method of introducing high-temperature tolerant varieties and the mitigation strategy of reducing chemical inputs affect the product price of rice in Japan. Finally, the last chapter proposes that robust strategies and policies from the relevant authorities are required to provide directions to stakeholders so that they can effectively and efficiently respond to climate change challenges.

Keywords

Adaptation and mitigation technology, agricultural sector, Asia, climate change, environmental information, food security, governance, legal sector, maritime time sector

Contents

List of Figures

List of Tables

Foreword

Climate Change Management: Special Topics in the Context of Asia is a necessary and much welcome volume on one of the most pressing matters facing our planet. The year 2017 has been partly defined by devastating climate-related disasters and many expect the severity of destruction, human tragedy, and dislocation to increase in severity as climate change continues. Although there is much more to study and learn about climate change overall, it is also important to focus on its specific impacts in different countries, regions, industries, ways of life, and political, economic, social, administrative, and institutional systems. Editor Huong Ha and the contributors to this book have done just that in excellent fashion with respect to several major issues and concern in Asia.

With the overall focus on climate change management, as the title indicates, chapters focus on industry, agriculture and food security, resources management, law, mitigation and adaptation technologies, and lessons from the Asian experience. While all these chapters make very important contributions to our knowledge base, I particularly welcome the attention the book gives to law and legal issues. Mitigating and adapting to climate change requires attention not only to science, economics, industry, agriculture, and other familiar topics, but also to legal regimes. And constructing these effectively to meet the many challenges ahead will take concerted country-by-country and worldwide efforts. Chapter 4 on "Legal Issues and Legal Framework with regard to Climate Change in the Context of the Maritime Industry in South Asia" by Shivani Raswan Pathania and Huong Ha and Chapter 5 on "The Legal Industry Response to Climate Change in Malaysia" by Oliva Tan Swee Leng are excellent contributions and examples of the kind of studies that are necessary to gain a better understanding of the multifold considerations that productive legal adaptation in the face of climate change must include.

The chapters in this outstanding volume address a broad range of topics that are both timely and urgent. They are authoritative and offer much to learn. The lessons they provide extend beyond Asia and can also substantially improve understanding of climate change problems and challenges in other regions. This is a book that should be widely read by all who seek to advance climate change management throughout the world.

—Prof David H. Rosenbloom
Chinese Thousand Talents Program Professor, Renmin University of China
Distinguished Professor of Public Administration
American University (Washington, DC)

Acknowledgments

It was impossible for this book to be completed without the support of contributors, the reviewers, the authors, family members, and friends. The editor takes pride in acknowledging the great role of the reviewers and the authors/contributors. The editor wishes to thank (i) the reviewers for their professional and constructive feedback which is valuable to the authors, (ii) the contributing authors for their cooperation during the revision stages, and (iii) Dr. Stanley Bruce Thomson for his exceptional and tireless support during the review and proofreading processes. Finally, the authors are very grateful for the advice and assistance from the editor(s) of BEP, USA.

Editor

Dr. Huong Ha

List of Reviewers

Dr. Misa Aoki (Nara Women's University, Japan)

Dr. Charlita Andales-Escano (Mindanao Development Authority, Philippines)

Dr. Kittinun Boonrod (Phetchaburi Rajabhat University, Thailand)

Prof. Dr. Tek Nath Dhakal (Tribhuvan University, Nepal)

Mr. Tarakeshwar Dhurjati (Grant Thornton, India)

Dr. Huong Ha (Singapore University of Social Sciences, Singapore)

Dr. Jak Jabes (University of Ottawa, Canada)

Prof. Dr. Neena Joseph (Institute of Management in Government, Regional Centre, Kochi, India)

Prof. Dr. Sarfraz Khawaja (Civil Services Academy, Lahore, Pakistan)

Prof. Dr. Sanjeev Kumar Mahajan (Himachal Pradesh University, India)

Prof. Dr. Steven Leibo (Russell Sage College, USA)

A/Prof. Dr. Ahmad Martadha Mohamed (Universiti Utara Malaysia, Malaysia)

Dr. Klinpratoonm Panyaping (Rajamangala University of Technology Lanna, Thailand)

Dr. Vidhyandika D. Perkasa (Centre for Strategic and International Studies, Indonesia)

Mr. Bigmal Raj Remi (Flinder University, Australia)

Prof. Dr. David Rosenbloom (American University, Washington DC, USA)

Dr. rer. nat. Claus-Peter Rückemann (Leibniz Universität Hannover and the Westfälische Wilhelms-Universität Münster, Germany)

A/Prof. Dr. Katsuhiro Sasuga (Tokai University Kanagawa-ken, Japan)

A/Prof. Dr. Isaias S. Sealza (Xavier University, Philippines)

A/Prof. Dr. Vinay Sharma (Indian Institute of Technology, Roorkee, Uttarakhand, India)

Mr. Ashok Kumar Singha (CTRAN, India)

Dr. Olivia Tan Swee Leng (Multimedia University, Malaysia)

Dr. Stanley Bruce Thomson (MacEwan University and University of Alberta in Edmonton, Alberta, Canada)

CHAPTER 1

Climate Change Management: Perspectives from Some Industries in the Context of Asia

Huong Ha and Hui Shan Loh

Introduction

The recent report of the Intergovernmental Panel on Climate Change (IPCC) on the assessment of climate change impacts, adaptation, and vulnerability explains that changes in climate have not only affected the natural and human systems across the countries in all continents, but they have also disturbed the socio-economic development (IPCC 2007, 2014a, b; Kim and Lim 2016). It has been noted that environmental degradation, environmental disasters, and climate change impact have gone beyond the control of any single country or any governance approach. Also, the current governance mechanisms have not yielded anticipated outcomes, and have not commendably addressed climate change-related issues at various levels, local, national, and international. Different countries have implemented different approaches to manage climate change, and different outcomes have been achieved. This has been evidenced via the assessment of countries' environmental performance. The recent negotiations in Paris in December 2015, with "tears of frustration and anger" pose new challenges to countries regarding achieving the target of emission reduction (AFP 2015, p. 10). Yale Center for Environmental Law and Policy and Center for International Earth Science Information Network (2014, 2016) have conducted research and established the Environmental Performance Index (EPI) rankings of 132 countries in 2014 and 180 in 2016. A few points are noted from the 2016 EPI rankings: (i) Only one country, Singapore, in the Asian region was in the strongest performers list, that is, top 20 countries; (ii) Only two Asian countries were classified in the top 60 countries; and (iii) 10 Asian countries were classified in the last 60 countries (Yale Center for Environmental Law and Policy and Center for International Earth Science Information Network 2016). India has been an emerging market and has been considered as a catalyst for economic change and development in the next decade together with China and other emerging economies (Ha 2014, 2016). However, China was ranked 109, and India was ranked 141 in 2016 (Yale Center for Environmental Law and Policy and Center for International Earth Science Information Network 2016), that is, belonging to the EPI's weakest performers list. Figures from the Climate Change Performance (CCP) Index 2015 and 2016 also indicate that different countries have produced different outcomes regarding climate change governance (Burck, Marten, and Bals 2015, 2016). Generally, most of Asian countries did not score well in terms of EPI ranking and the CCP Index. In other words, while several nations have been pursuing national initiatives and participating in some common agenda to slow down the process of climate change mitigation, and/or adaptation to its consequences, this task has absolutely become a real challenge for all relevant stakeholders, including government, the private sector, civil society, and individuals in different economic sectors in different countries.

Given the fact that out of the 10 largest CO_2 emitters, five of them, namely India, Indonesia, Japan, Korea, and China, are from Asia (see Climate Change Performance Index 2016 by Burck, Marten, and Bals 2016), it is justified that research on climate change governance in Asia should receive more attention. Nevertheless, most of the studies on climate change governance examined issues at the macro level, that is, insufficient research on climate change has been done at the micro level. Thus, this volume aims to close the gap by including research papers covering issues at the micro level or industry level. This volume also incorporates the views of stakeholders from different political actors (government, private, and civil society), different economic sectors, and from various disciplines (environment, agriculture, urban development, tourism, etc.).

Obviously, research on the adverse effects of climate change have transcended various areas and disciplines as well as cross-sectorial, cross-national and cross-continental, new and innovative approaches to manage and govern climate change are imperative to mitigate and adapt to climate change impacts at various levels, especially at the industry level. Thus, the objectives of this edited volume are to (i) examine how different industries manage climate change-related issues, and respond to climate change impacts, in their current capacities and resources; (ii) examine different forms of process innovations in different sectors required to mitigate climate change and adapt to its impacts; and (iii) discuss innovative approaches and mechanisms to enhance the public awareness of the adverse effects of climate change.

The five chapters, excluding the introduction and the conclusion chapters, included in this volume are contributed by academics and practitioners from different countries and from different disciplines and various research interests. These chapters cover topics about issues and impact of climate change, and approaches to climate change management in some industries in the context of Asia.

Issues and Challenges Associated with Climate Change and Climate Change Governance in the Context of Asian Countries

Asian countries have faced common issues of climate change, for example, environment-related problems, such as temperature increases, increase in global sea level, changes in bio- and eco-systems, and climate hazards, such as, cyclones, typhoons, hurricanes, drought, floods, etc. (Ward et al. 2016; Zickgraf et al. 2016). Other examples include (i) the diminishing of various species and local landraces and (ii) the decrease in agricultural productivity and yield (Food and Agriculture Organization of the United Nations 2008, 2016; Kang, Khan, and Ma 2009). Agricultural productive has been declining over the time due to the fluctuation of rainfall, the loss of soil fertility, leading to (i) lack of inputs, (ii) shortage of labor due to rural-urban migration, and (iii) the occurrence of epidemic and the plague of pests and many other outbreaks (Knox et al. 2012; Malla 2009; Manandhar et al. 2011). Apart from the ecological impacts, the economic impacts of climate change have also been observed, including "loss of agricultural revenue and additional costs for managing water resources, coastlines, and disease and other health risks will be a drag on economic activity" (International Fund for Agricultural Development 2008, p. 2). In addition, climate change has also entailed adverse effects on food securities and gender (Goh 2012; UNDP 2012; Cook 2016).

Women in less developed countries, especially in the rural areas, are vulnerable to climate change impact since they depend much on limited local natural resources for their incomes and livelihood. Limited access to resources, less power to make decision, and limited mobility make these women disproportionately affected by climate change (Alam, Bhatia, and Mawby 2015; Bossuet and Huyer 2016). Besides, the increase in migration flow from the rural areas to urban areas has also created labor crisis in the remote areas which, in turn, intensify the workload burden on women. Hence, gender is a critical policy issue of climate change in the context of Asia.

The Food and Agriculture Organization of the United Nations (FAO) (2008) affirms that there is a strong indirect or negative correlation between climate change and food security. The increase in the amount of GHG emission, the wide spread of deforestation due to burning of fossil fuels to "meet increasing energy demand, and the spread of intensive agriculture to meet increasing food demand," and the changes in weather conditions due to global warming have seriously impacted "the four dimensions of food security: food availability, food accessibility, food utilization and food system stability" (The Food and Agriculture Organization of the United Nations 2008, p. 1). Thus, there are good reasons for us to embark on research on how climate change mitigation and adaptation strategies and technologies affect agricultural production. Japan has emerged as one of the interesting cases with regards to technology and food security given the emphasis on environmental friendly agricultural and organic farming methods (Moreno-Peñaranda 2011). There is a strong correlation between mitigation technologies and the supply, the quality, the harvest year of agricultural products, and these, in turn, affect the price of such products, such as rice (Sustainable Development Solutions Network 2013). Scientifically, in order to adapt to climate change, new varieties of agricultural products which have good quality, superior taste, and high yields should be developed. The costs of investment and implementation of a mixture of mitigation and adaptation technologies would be incorporated in the product prices which have been explored in Japan. The case of Japan can be scalable to other countries with regards to the adoption of new technologies to improve the productivity, the quality, and the varieties of agricultural products in order to respond to the food security and food crisis due to climate change (Grafton, Williams, and Jiang 2016).

Another challenge of climate change-related issue is the knowledge and resource management in the information age (Sala 2010; Shi et al. 2016). Information technology is important to record, transform, broadcast, and retrieve relevant information in a climate change management process (Pulwarty and Verdin 2013). Hence, it is essential to explore different information systems and ways to manage "knowledge and action at the relevant scales for decision making in response to a changing climate" (Pulwarty and Sivakumar 2014, p. 14).

Finally, an increase in global trade has increased the volume of shipping via sea, which has led to a high amount of global carbon dioxide (CO_2) emissions and water contamination due to discharge of oil, pesticides, hazardous wastes, and industrial effluents (Klein 2009). Jurisdiction and legal complication is unavoidable when climate change-related issues, such as the introduction and implementation of carbon tax and carbon trading, and climate change-related disputes in the maritime sector, occur at both the national and international levels (Conefrey et al. 2008). Apparently, there is substantial evidence to include these issues in this book. The next section will discuss how different industries manage and govern climate change impact.

Governance of climate change is usually associated with institutional planning and arrangements, key players and actors, stakeholder management, systems, instruments, and legal requirements and parameters that directly or indirectly affect the process of climate change management (Djalante, Holley, and Thomalla 2011; Ha 2016; Holley et al. 2011; United Nations Climate Change Secretariat 2014). Practically, no single actor or sector has sufficient knowledge or potential to dominate the governance process of climate change given the nature, the scope of scale of climate change impact (Rhodes 1996, 2007; Kooiman and Jentoft 2009;

Visscher, Laubscher, and Chan 2016). There is interdependence among actors in different levels, that is, international, national, and industry levels. As such, though government is normally responsible for governing public issues, such as climate change mitigation and adaptation, many countries have adopted top-down governing approaches to embrace a wider range of non-state actors from economic and social communities, including industry and professional associations, statutory boards, and nongovernmental organizations (Forino, Meding, and Brewer 2015; Rotter et al. 2016). Given the multifaceted and complicated nature of climate change, climate change management should not only be examined at the internal and national levels, but should also be explored in different contexts and at the industry level. Thus, it is justified for us to discuss how different industries have responded to climate change impact in the second part of this book.

Last but not least, growing concerns about the current and potential impacts of climate change in these countries have escalated the multilevel debates over what has been, could be, and should be done to address the potential socio-economic and environmental impacts of climate change in a more effective and efficient manner. From this perspective, there is a need to engage all groups of stakeholders in the governance process of climate change (Gardner et al. 2009; Akompab et al. 2013; Al-zu'bi 2016). The public will demonstrate pro-environmental behaviors if they have good understanding of climate change and its adverse impacts (Hung and Kim 2014; Masud et al. 2015). According to the study by Lee et al. (2015), education is the single strongest factor affecting climate change awareness, and sound understanding of the root causes of climate change is the strongest predictor of climate change risk perceptions. Given the importance of education pertaining to climate change, it is strongly recommended that stakeholders should receive climate change-related education as early as possible (Gam-ad, Martin, and Stortz 2016; Shaw 2016).

An Overview of the Chapters

This edited book starts with "*Impact of Climate Change on Agriculture and Food Security from Socio-Economic Perspectives in Nepal*" (Chapter 2) by Remi, Star, and Paudval. The authors explain that agricultural and food security in Nepal, similarly to any other countries in the South Asian region, has adversely been impacted by climate change. According to the authors, climate change-related variables along with socio-economic factors directly impact the decrease in agricultural production (Kang et al. 2009; Nyuor et al. 2016). The increasing reduction in land holding size has made poor households more vulnerable, especially when natural disasters occur. For example, floods in Bangesaal, Nepal destroyed crops and washed away agriculture land. The findings suggest that climate change has complicated and accelerated the existing problems associated with agricultural and food security in Nepal.

Chapter 3 continues the conceptualization of an interdisciplinary approach with Rückemann examining the creation of long-term multidisciplinary knowledge resources in order to respond to climate change-related issues. Rückemann discussed how structures and classification in the context of High-End Computing (HEC) can be used for the management of environmental and climatological information, and knowledge management in various disciplines and industries (Leitão, Inden, and Rückemann 2013). Overall, the chapter is unique since the approach is not normally found in the literature regarding climate change.

In Chapter 4, Pathania and Ha analyze climate change impact on the maritime industry, and the extent to which the current legal framework can contribute to climate change mitigation and adaptation in the context of South Asia. The authors explain that although regulations and laws have been introduced, such as the UNCLOS, these legal instruments appear to be inadequate to address the complicated and unexpected challenges of climate change in the maritime sphere (Michel 2012; Michel and Sticklor 2012; UNEP 2016).

The next chapter focuses on law and climate change. According to Leng (Chapter 5) some impacts of climate change include the intensive rivalry for limited resources, territorial change, disruption to trade patterns, food insecurity, a reduction of productivity in the agricultural, forestry, and fishery sectors (Barnes and Breslow 2003; Food and Agriculture Organization of the United Nations 2008; Nachmany et al. 2016). This chapter examines how the legal industry in Malaysia responds to climate change in a manner which can resolve global issues, and at the same time, contribute to develop and sustain the national economy.

How the price of rice in Japan is affected by mitigation and adaptation technologies in rice production due to climate change is discussed in Chapter 6. Aoki explains that the choice of adaption technologies is crucial since such technologies will affect agricultural product pricing. The climate change adaptive method involving in high-temperature tolerant varieties of rice, and the mitigation strategy of reducing chemical inputs, such as fertilizers and pesticides, are the center of the discussion in this chapter (Patle, Badyopadhyay, and Kumar 2014; UNFCC 2006).

Conclusion

International and national climate policy components account for 20 percent of the total weight of the CCP Index researched by Germanwatch and CAN (Burck et al. 2015, 2016). This reinforces the importance of governance to improve CCP. Since the impact of climate change has gone beyond the conventional governance approaches and transcended research fields and disciplines and national boundaries, innovative governance approaches to effectively and efficiently manage climate change and its impact should be explored not only at regional and national levels, but also at the local and sectorial levels.

Generally, governance of climate change is a dynamic, complex, and multidimensional process, embracing various groups of stakeholders in different sectors. Both developed and developing countries have faced multiple challenges when discharging their duty to tackle climate change-related issues and reducing the vulnerability of various stakeholder groups. However, the current governance arrangements, systems, instruments, and processes to mitigate and adapt to climate change exhibit many shortcomings (Dhakhal and Ha 2013; Ha 2013; Ha and Dhakal 2013; Jang, McSparren, and Rashchupkina 2016). Thus, they should be reviewed and modified in order to respond to the changing external and internal environments at all levels. In short, the above chapters emphasize the importance of searching for more holistic and comprehensive governance approaches to address the current and future challenges associated with climate change.

This volume provides better insights to policy and decision makers, researchers, and those who are interested in the topics so that they can have a better understanding of (i) the relationship between climate change and information, gender, legal issues, agriculture; and (ii) how some industries have responded to the adverse effect of climate change.

Some suggestions to address the agricultural problems include proactive initiatives, agricultural reform and legal enforcement are required in order to facilitate the access of farmers to better weather forecasting equipment and information. An interdisciplinary research approach to address issues associated with climate change is important since it can meet the needs of different groups of stakeholders, including academic researchers, policy makers, practitioners, and communities at the grass-root level. Participatory approaches of governance that embrace all groups of stakeholders and actors in different political sectors may enhance the capacity of stakeholders to meet the challenges of climate change at all levels. Apparently, public education has been proposed to be one of the key mechanisms to enhance the public awareness of environmental problems and climate change.

Finally, one of the limitations of this book is its inability to cover all climate change-related issues and all industries due to resource and time constraints. Thus, further research should cover other climate change-related issues and other economic sectors.

References

AFB. 2015. "Tears Flow, Fatigue Takes Hold as Negotiators Approach Finish Line." *Today*, p. 10. December 11.

Akompab, D.A., P. Bi, S. Williams, A. Saniotis, I.A. Walker, and M. Augoustinos. 2013. "Engaging Stakeholders in an Adaptation Process: Governance and Institutional Arrangements in Heat-Health Policy Development in Adelaide, Australia." *Mitigation and Adaptation Strategies for Global Change* 18, no. 7, pp. 1001–18.

Alam, M., R. Bhatia, and B. Mawby. 2015. *Women and Climate Change: Impact and Agency in Human Rights, Security, and Economic Development.* Washington, DC: Georgetown Institute for Women, Peace and Security.

Al-zu'bi, M. 2016. "Jordan's Climate Change Governance Framework: From Silos to an Intersectoral Approach." *Environment Systems and Decisions* 36, no. 3, 277–301. doi:10.1007/s10669-016-9602-9

Barnes, P., and M. Breslow. 2003. "The Sky Trust: The Battle for Atmospheric Scarcity Rent." In *Natural Assets: Democratizing Environmental Ownership*, eds. J. Boyce and B.G. Shelley, 135–49. Washington, DC: Island Press.

Bossuet, J., and S. Huyer. 2016. *Gender and Climate Change Policy After COP21.* Frederiksberg: CCAFS Program, University of Copenhagen.

Burck, J., F. Marten, and C. Bals. 2015. *The Climate Change Performance Index Results 2015.* Bonn, Berlin, and Brussels: Germanwatch and Climate Action Network Europe (CAN).

Burck, J., F. Marten, and C. Bals. 2016. *The Climate Change Performance Index Results 2015.* Bonn, Berlin, and Brussels: Germanwatch and Climate Action Network Europe (CAN).

Conefrey, T., J.F. Gerald, L.M. Valeri, and R.S.J. Tol. 2008. "The Impact of a Carbon Tax on Economic Growth and Carbon Dioxide Emissions in Ireland." Papers WP251. Dublin: Economic and Social Research Institute (ESRI).

Cook, G. 2016. *Global Stories from the Nexus of Gender and Climate Change Vulnerability.* Washington, DC: Environmental Change and Security Program Woodrow Wilson International Center for Scholars.

Dhakal, T.N., and H. Ha. 2013. "Responses to Climate Change—Who is Responsible? A Conclusion." In *Governance approaches to mitigation of and adaptation to climate change in Asia,* eds. H. Ha and T.N. Dhakal, 267–72. London: Palgrave Mcmillan.

Djalante, R., C. Holley, and F. Thomalla. 2011. "Adaptive Governance and Managing Resilience to Natural Hazards." *International Journal of Disaster Risk Science* 2, no. 4, pp. 1–14.

European Environment Agency. 2016. *Analysis of Key Trends and Drivers in Greenhouse Gas Emissions in the EU between 1990 and 2014.* Copenhagen: European Environment Agency.

Food and Agriculture Organization of the United Nations. 2008. *Climate Change and Food Security: A Framework Document.* Rome: Food and Agriculture Organization of the United Nations.

Food and Agriculture Organization of the United Nations. 2016. *Climate Change and Food Security: Risks and Responses.* Rome: Food and Agriculture Organization of the United Nations.

Forino, G., J.V. Meding, and G.J. Brewer. 2015. "A Conceptual Governance Framework for Climate Change Adaptation and Disaster Risk Reduction Integration." *International Journal of Disaster Risk Science* 6, no. 4, pp. 372–84.

Gardner, J., A.M. Dowd, C. Mason, and P. Ashworth. 2009. "A Framework for Stakeholder Engagement on Climate Adaptation." CSIRO Climate Adaptation Flagship Working paper No. 3. CSIRO website http://csiro.au/resources/CAF-working-papers.html

Goh, A.H.X. 2012. "A Literature Review of the Gender-Differentiated Impacts of Climate Change on Women's and Men's Assets and Well-Being in Developing Countries." CAPRi Working Paper No. 106. Washington, DC: International Food Policy Research Institute.

Grafton, R.Q., J. Williams, and Q. Jiang. 2016. "Food Security: Asia's Critical Balancing Act." East Asia Forum, Retrieved from http://eastasiaforum. org/2016/02/02/food-security-asias-critical-balancing-act/

Ha, H. 2013. "Climate Change Governance: The Singapore Case." In *Governance Approaches to Mitigation and Adaptation of Climate Change in Asia,* eds. H. Ha and T.N. Dhakal, 182–99. London: Palgrave Mcmillan.

Ha, H. 2014. "Land Use and Disaster Governance in Asia: An Introduction." In *Land and Disaster Management Strategies in Asia*, ed. H. Ha, 1–14. New Delhi: Springer.

Ha, H. 2016. "Governance Framework for Humanitarian and Disaster Response in ASEAN." Middle East Institute, Retrieved from http://mei.edu/content/ map/governance-framework-humanitarian-assistance-and-disaster-response-asean

Ha, H., and T.N. Dhakal. 2013. "Governance Approaches to Mitigation of and Adaptation to Climate Change in Asia: An Introduction." In *Governance Approaches to Mitigation of and Adaptation to Climate Change in Asia*, eds. H. Ha and T.N. Dhakal, 1–12. London: Palgrave Mcmillan.

Holley, C., and D. Sinclair. 2011. "Collaborative Governance and Adaptive Management: (Mis)Applications to Groundwater Salinity and Run-Off." *The Australasian Journal of Natural Resources Law and Policy* 14, no. 1, pp. 37–69.

Hung, C.C., and I.K. Kim. 2014. "Climate Change Resilience and Public Education in Response to Hydrologic Extremes in Singapore." *British Journal of Environmental and Climate Change* 4, no. 3, pp. 328–54.

IPCC (Intergovernmental Panel on Climate Change). 2007. *IPCC Fourth Assessment Report: Climate Change 2007*. Geneva: The IPCC Secretariat.

IPCC (Intergovernmental Panel on Climate Change). 2014a. *Climate Change 2014: Synthesis Report. Contribution of Working Groups I, II and III to the Fifth Assessment Report of the Intergovernmental Panel on Climate Change* [Core Writing Team, R.K. Pachauri and L.A. Meyer (eds.)]. Geneva: The IPCC Secretariat.

IPCC (Intergovernmental Panel on Climate Change). 2014b. "Summary for Policymakers." In *Climate Change 2014: Impacts, Adaptation, and Vulnerability*, 1–32. Part A: Global and Sectoral Aspects. Contribution of Working Group II to the Fifth Assessment Report of the Intergovernmental Panel on Climate Change [Field, C.B., V.R. Barros, D.J. Dokken, K.J. Mach, M.D. Mastrandrea, T.E. Bilir, M. Chatterjee, K.L. Ebi, Y.O. Estrada, R.C. Genova, B. Girma, E.S. Kissel, A.N. Levy, S. MacCracken, P.R. Mastrandrea, and L.L. White (eds.)]. Cambridge, UK and New York, NY: Cambridge University Press.

Jang, J., J. McSparren, and Y. Rashchupkina. 2016. "Global Governance: Present and Future." *Palgrave Communications* 2, 15045. doi:10.1057/ palcomms.2015.45

Kang, Y., S. Khan, and X. Ma. 2009. "Climate Change Impacts on Crop Yield, Crop Water Productivity and Food Security—A Review." *Progress in Natural Science* 19, no. 12, 1665–74. http://sciencedirect.com/science/article/pii/S1002007109002810

Kim, D., and U. Lim. 2016. "Urban Resilience in Climate Change Adaptation: A Conceptual Framework." *Sustainability* 8, 405. doi:10.3390/su8040405

Klein, R.A. 2009. *Getting a Grip on Cruise Ship Pollution*. Amsterdam: Friends of the Earth.

Knox, J., T. Hess, A. Daccache, and T. Wheeler. 2012. "Climate Change Impacts on Crop Productivity in Africa and South Asia." *Environmental Research Letters* 7, no. 3, pp. 1–8.

Kooiman, J., and S. Jentoft. 2009. "Meta-Governance: Values, Norms and Principles, and the Making of Hard Choices." *Public Administration* 87, no. 4, pp. 818–36.

Lee, T.M., E.M. Markowitz, P.D. Howe, C.Y. Ko, and A.A. Leiserowitz. 2015. "Predictors of Public Climate Change Awareness and Risk Perception Around the World." *Nature Climate Change* 5, pp. 1014–20.

Leitão, P., U. Inden, and C.P. Rückemann. November 2013. "Parallelising Multi-agent Systems for High Performance Computing." In *Proceedings of the Third International Conference on Advanced Communications and Computation (INFOCOMP 2013)*. Lisbon, Portugal. XPS Press. Retrieved from http://thinkmind.org/download.php?articleid=infocomp_2013_1_10_10055

Lyseen, K., C. Nøhr, E.M. Sørensen, O. Gudes, E.M. Geraghty, N.T. Shaw, and C. Bivona-Tellez. 2014. "A Review and Framework for Categorizing Current Research and Development in Health Related Geographical Information Systems (GIS) Studies." *Yearbook of Medical Informatics* 9, no. 1, pp. 110–24.

Malla, G. 2009. "Climate Change and its Impact on Nepalese Agriculture." *Journal of Agriculture and Environment* 9, pp. 62–71.

Manandhar, S., D. Vogt, P.R. Sylvain, and K. Futuba. 2011. "Adapting Cropping Systems to Climate Change in Nepal: A Cross-Regional Study of Farmers' Perception and Practices." *Regional Environmental Change* 11, no. 2, pp. 335–48.

Masud, M.M., R. Akhtar, R. Afroz, A.Q. Al-Amin, and F.B. Kari. 2015. "Pro-Environmental Behavior and Public Understanding of Climate Change." *Mitigation and Adaptation Strategies for Global Change* 20, no. 4, pp. 591–600.

Michel, D. 2012. "Environmental Pressures in the Indian Ocean." In *Indian Ocean Rising: Maritime Security and Policy Challenges*, eds. D. Michel and R. Sticklor, 113–29. Washington, DC: Stimson.

Michel, D., and R. Sticklor. 2012. "Indian Ocean Rising: Maritime and Security Policy Challenges." In *Indian Ocean Rising: Maritime Security and Policy Challenges*, eds. D. Michel and R. Sticklor, 9–22. Washington, DC: Stimson.

Moreno-Peñaranda, R. 2011. *Japan's Urban Agriculture: Cultivating Sustainability and Well-being*. Tokyo: United Nations University.

Nachmany, M., S. Fankhauser, J. Davidová, N. Kingsmill, T. Landesman, H. Roppongi, P. Schleifer, J. Setzer, A. Sharman, C.S. Singleton, J. Sundaresan, and T. Townshend. 2016. *Climate Change Legislation in Malaysia: An Excerpt from the 2015 Global Climate Legislation Study A Review of Climate Change Legislation in 99 Countrie*s. London: Grantham Research Institute on Climate Change and the Environment, The Global Legislators Organisation, and Inter-Parliamentary Union.

Nyuor, A.B., E. Donkor, R. Aidoo, S.S. Buah, J.B. Naab, S.K. Nutsugah, J. Bayala, and R. Zougmoré. 2016. "Economic Impacts of Climate Change on Cereal Production: Implications for Sustainable Agriculture in Northern Ghana." *Sustainability* 8, pp. 724–50.

Patle, G.T., K.K. Badyopadhyay, and M. Kumar. 2014. "An Overview of Organic Agriculture: A Potential Strategy for Climate Change Mitigation." *Journal of Applied and Natural Science* 6, no. 2, pp. 872–79.

Pulwarty, R.S., and M.V.K. Sivakumar. June 2014. "Information Systems in a Changing Climate: Early Warnings and Drought Risk Management." *Weather and Climate Extremes* 3, pp. 14–21.

Pulwarty, R., and J. Verdin. 2013. "Crafting Early Warning Information Systems: The Case of Drought." In *Measuring Vulnerability to Natural Hazards: Towards Disaster Resilient Societies*, ed. Birkmann. 2nd ed. Tokyo: United Nations University Press.

Rhodes, R.A.W. 1996. "The New Governance: Governing Without Government." *Political Studies* 44, no. 4, pp. 652–67.

Rhodes, R.A.W. 2007. "Understanding Governance: Ten Years on." *Organization Studies* 28, no. 8, pp. 1243–64.

Rothballer, C., S. Castaqnino, and P. Gerbert. 2016. *What's the Future of the Construction Industry?* Geneva: World Economic Forum.

Rotter, M., E. Hoffmann, A. Pechan, and R. Stecker. 2016. "Competing Priorities: How Actors and Institutions Influence Adaptation of the German Railway System." *Climatic Change* 137, no. 3, pp. 609–23.

Sala, S. 2010. *The Role of Information and Communication Technologies for Community-Based Adaptation to Climate Change*. Rome: Food and Agriculture Organization of the United Nations.

Shaw, S. 2016. "It's Time to Teach Climate Change in School. Here's how." *The Guardian News*. Retrieved September 19 from https://theguardian.com/commentisfree/2014/sep/19/its-time-to-teach-climate-change-in-school-heres-how

Shi, J., V.H.M. Visschers, M. Siegrist, and J. Arval. 2016. "Knowledge as a Driver of Public Perceptions About Climate Change Reassessed." *Nature Climate Change* 6, pp. 759–62.

SDSN (Sustainable Development Solutions Network). 2013. *Solutions for Sustainable Agriculture and Food Systems: Technical Report for the Post-2015 Development Agenda.* Paris and New York: Sustainable Development Solutions Network.

IFAD (International Fund for Agricultural Development). 2008. *Climate Change Impacts in the Asia/Pacific Region.* Rome: The International Fund for Agricultural Development (IFAD).

UNDP (United Nations Development Programme). 2012. *Gender, Climate Change and Food Security.* New York, NY: UNDP.

UNEP (United Nations Environment Programme). 2009. *Building and Climate Change: Summary for Decision-Makers.* Milan: United Nations Environmental Programme and Sustainable Buildings and Climate Initiative (SBCI).

UNEP (United Nations Environment Programme). 2016. *GEO-6 Regional Assessment for Asia and the Pacific.* Nairobi: United Nations Environment Programme.

UNFCCC (United Nations Framework Convention on Climate Change). 2006. *Technologies for Adaptation to Climate Change.* Bonn, Germany: Climate.

United Nations. 2015. *Policy Integration in Government in Pursuit of the Sustainable Development Goals.* New York, NY: United Nations.

Yale Center for Environmental Law & Policy and Center for International Earth Science Information Network. 2014. *2014 Environmental Performance Index.* New Haven, CT and Palisades, NY: Yale Center for Environmental Law & Policy.

Yale Center for Environmental Law & Policy and Center for International Earth Science Information Network. 2016. *2016 Environmental Performance Index.* New Haven, CT and Palisades, NY: Yale Center for Environmental Law & Policy.

Visscher, H., J. Laubscher, and E. Chan. 2016. "Building Governance and Climate Change: Roles for Regulation and Related Polices." *Building Research & Information* 44, nos. 5–6, pp. 461–67.

Ward, R.D., D.A. Friess, R.H. Day, and R.A. MacKenzie. 2016. "Impacts of Climate Change on Mangrove Ecosystems: A Region by Region Overview." *Ecohealth and Sustainability* 2, no. 4, p. e01211.

World Bank. December 2010. "Part III Cities' Contribution to Climate Change." *Cities and Climate Change: An Urgent Agenda* 10, pp. 14–32.

Zickgraf, C., S. Vigil, F. de Longueville, P. Ozer, and F. Gemenne. 2016. *The Impact of Vulnerability and Resilience to Environmental Changes on Mobility Patterns in West Africa.* Washington, DC: Knomad.

Further/Suggested Reading

Bacchi, C. 2010. "Policy and Discourse: Challenging the Construction of Affirmative Action as Preferential Treatment." *Journal of European Public Policy* 11, no. 1, pp. 128–46.

Brody, A., J. Demetriades, and E. Esplen. 2008. *Gender and Climate Change: Mapping the Linkages: A Scoping Study on Knowledge and Gaps.* Brighton: Institute of Development Studies.

Dodman, D. 2009. "Blaming Cities for Climate Change? An Analysis of Urban Greenhouse Gas Emission Inventories." *Environment and Urbanisation* 21, no. 1, pp. 185–201.

Doelle, M. 2009. "The Climate Change Regime and the Arctic Region." *Climate Governance in the Arctic Environment & Policy* 50, no. 2, pp. 27–50.

Elbeih, S.F. 2015. "An Overview of Integrated Remote Sensing and GIS for Groundwater Mapping in Egypt." *Ain Shams Engineering Journal* 6, no. 1, pp. 1–15.

Food and Agriculture Organization of the United Nations. 2016. *Climate Change and Food Security: Risks and Responses.* Rome: Food and Agriculture Organization of the United Nations.

Ha, H., and T.N. Dhakal, eds. 2013. *Governance Approaches to Mitigation and Adaptation of Climate Change in Asia.* London, UK: Palgrave Mcmillan.

Lorenzoni, I., S. Nicholson-Cole, and L. Whitmarsh. 2007. "Barriers Perceived to Engaging with Climate Change Among the UK Public and their Policy Implications." *Global Environmental Change* 17, no. 3, pp. 445–59.

Narayanan, K., and S.K. Sahu. 2016. "Effects of Climate Change on Household Economy and Adaptive Responses Among Agricultural Households in Eastern Coast of India." *Current Science* 110, no. 7, pp. 1240–50.

Nishimura, T., K. Matsushita, and T. Fujie. 2012. "Consumer Willingness to Buy Biodiversity-Friendly Agricultural Products: The Role of Consumer Characteristics and Knowledge." *Journal of Food System Research* 18, no. 4, pp. 403–14.

Peters, G.P. 2010. "Carbon Footprints and Embodied Carbon at Multiple Scales." *Current Opinion in Environmental Sustainability* 2, pp. 245–50.

Rama Rao, C.A., B.K. Raju, A.M. Subba Rao, K.V. Rao, V.M. Rao, K. Ramachandran, and C. Srinivasa Rao. 2016. "A District Level Assessment of Vulnerability of Indian Agriculture to Climate Change." *Current Science* 110, no. 10, pp. 1939–46.

Reed, M., A. Graves, N. Dandy, H. Posthumus, K. Hubacek, J. Morris, C. Prell, C. Quinn, and L. Stringer. 2009. "Who's in and Why? A Typology of Stakeholder Analysis Methods for Natural Resource Management." *Journal of Environmental Management* 90, pp. 1933–49.

Rekadwad, B.N., and C.N. Khobragade. December 2016. "Is the Increase in Oil Pollution a Possibility of the Presence of Diverse Microorganisms? An Experimental Dataset on Oil Prevalent Areas of Goa, India." *Data in Brief* 9, pp. 8–12.

Rosenzweig, C., and M.L. Parry. 1994. "Potential Impact of Climate Change on World Food Supply." *Nature* 367, no. 6459, pp. 133–38.

Shrestha, A.B., C.P. Wake, P.A. Mayewski, and J.E. Dibb. 1999. "Maximum Temperature Trends in the Himalaya and its Vicinity: An Analysis Based on Temperature Records from Nepal for the Period 1971–94." *Journal of Climate* 12, no. 9, pp. 2775–86.

Tashmin, N. 2016. "Can Climate Finance in Bangladesh be Helpful in Making Transformational Change in Ecosystem Management?" *Environmental Systems Research* 5, p. 2.

The Asia Foundation. 2012. *A Situation Analysis of Climate Change Adaptation Initiatives in Bangladesh*. Dhaka: The Asia Foundation.

UNEP (United Nations Environment Programme). 2006. *Raising Awareness of Climate Change a Handbook for Government Focal Points*. Geneva: UNEP.

United Nations. 2015. *Policy Integration in Government in Pursuit of the Sustainable Development Goals*. New York, NY: United Nations.

CHAPTER 2

Impact of Climate Change on Agriculture and Food Security from Socio-Economic Perspectives in Nepal

Bimal Raj Regmi and Apar Paudyal

Introduction

The extreme weather variability and changes in South Asia has put the agriculture farming system at risk and uncertainty. As the farming system is largely dependent on weather and practiced in natural environment, Nepalese agriculture is a climate sensitive sector because of the close relationship between crop production and climatic variables like temperature and rainfall. It is projected that climate change will impact food security by the middle of 21st century, with the largest numbers of food-insecure people located in South Asia (Hijioka et al. 2014). A systematic review projected mean changes in yield by 16 percent for maize and 11 percent for sorghum by the 2050s across South Asia (Knox et al. 2012).

Nepal is highly exposed to climate change because of its fragile landscape, poor socio-economic growth, and increased weather variability and change (NCVST 2009). The temperature in Nepal has increased rapidly at a much faster rate than the global average. The study carried out by Practical Action showed that over a period of 30 years (1976 to 2005), the trend of observed warming for Nepal was approximately 0.5°C per decade, driven by higher warming at higher altitudes (Practical Action

2009). This is significantly higher than the global average trend (closer to 0.1°C per decade) (IPCC 2014). There have also been changes in precipitation, including increases in extreme rainfall events and water-related disasters such as drought and flooding.

Over two-third (66.5 percent) of the population of Nepal is employed by the agriculture sector. The average land-holding size per household is 0.7 ha and the overall share of irrigated land area is around 54 percent (CBS 2011). So by nature, the farmers in Nepal are small holders and the agriculture largely depends on natural climate. The impact of climate change is expected to increase both risk and vulnerability of the agriculture system leading to crop failure and loss of productivity (Alam and Regmi 2004). The recent study shows that in the longer term (mid-century and beyond), due to climate change, there will be high overall net loss to the agriculture sector, which is equivalent to 0.8 percent of current annual Gross Domestic Product (GDP) (Intergrated Development Society Nepal (IDS-Nepal), Practical Action (PA), and Global Climate Adaptation Partnership (GCCA) 2014).

The implementation of climate change responses in agriculture sector in Nepal is lagging behind. One of the major reasons is due to lack of relevant capacity as well as information and knowledge on the scale and magnitude of climate change impact in the agriculture sector (Malla 2009). This is why the government research and extension system is inadequate to take necessary measures to deal with climate extremity and impact. Likewise, due to lack of information and knowledge base, it has been difficult for the donors, civil society, and even government implementing agencies to decide on the priorities for agriculture sector (Regmi et al. 2009).

This chapter fills the information and knowledge gap in agriculture sector in terms of outlining climate change implications for agriculture production and food security. The chapter particularly investigates the vulnerability of agriculture-dependent communities by analyzing their exposure, sensitivity, and adaptive capacity and identifying factors that shapes the capacity to respond. The outcome of this chapter is relevant for the government of Nepal and Nepali stakeholders in particular to understand the impact of climate change in agriculture and food security in Nepal. This understanding will further guide policy makers and practitioners to develop policy and strategies to strategically deal with food security issues at the local and national level.

Climate Change and Agriculture in Nepal

Agriculture is both the source of greenhouse gas (GHG) emissions as well as major sector that is impacted by climate change (Hijioka et al. 2014). The direct and indirect GHG emissions from food systems account for between 19 and 29 percent of the total global anthropogenic emissions (Vermeulen, Campbell, and Ingram 2012). In Nepal, the third national communication report projects that agriculture is the major source of GHG emissions in Nepal. Within the agriculture emissions, 28.2 percent of the GHG emission comes from unregulated fertilizer and pesticide use (MoSTE 2015).

The majority of the population in Nepal is dependent on agriculture for their livelihood. As argued before, the recent census data shows that 66.5 percent of the population is employed by the agriculture sector (CBS 2011). As large population in rural areas of Nepal are dependent on climate sensitive sectors like agriculture, impacts of climate change is expected to increase both risk and vulnerability of the agriculture system leading to crop failure and loss of productivity (Biggs et al. 2013; Alam and Regmi 2004). The recent study shows that in the longer-term (mid-century and beyond), due to climate change there will be high overall net loss to the agriculture sector, which is equivalent to 0.8 percent of current annual GDP (IDS-Nepal et al. 2014).

Weather and climate-specific implications exist in the farming system in Nepal which depends on rain-fed system and specifically on the monsoon rainfall (IDS-Nepal et al. 2014). Over the past years, the delay in monsoon season experienced in Nepal has changed the cropping pattern and crop maturity period. It has delayed the planting and harvesting season by a month, which has in turn affected rotation practices. Poudel and Kotani (2012) referred that an increase in the variance of both temperature and rainfall has adverse effects on crop productions in general. The impact of erratic rainfall and monsoon behavior is also reported by other researches in Nepal (Chaudhury et al. 2016; Sapkota et al. 2011; Gentle and Maraseni 2012).

The impact of climate change is leading to increased food insecurity in Nepal. Over 10 percent of production decline is caused by climate induced disasters and lack of adaptation action. Due to drought in 2006 only, 11 percent of rice yield and 7 percent of wheat yield losses were recorded in Nepal. A drought in the Eastern region of Nepal decreased the rice production by 30 percent in 2006 and heavy flooding in the mid-western and far-western regions in 2006 and 2008 destroyed crops in many places (WFP 2009; Oxfam 2009). The extreme drought conditions in the mid- and far-western region of Nepal in 2015-2016 have impacted more than 400,000 households directly. According to the monitoring and analysis, 150,000 people has are estimated to be affected in 59 VDCs (Village Development Committees) in five districts which is nearly 90 percent of all the population in this area.

The future projection of temperature increase shows more alarming situation for the agriculture sector in Nepal. Due to extreme weather conditions, the rice yield is projected to decrease by 10 percent in the Terai region by 2070s (IDS-Nepal et al. 2014). The third national communication report of Nepal (in the process) mentions that around 1.6 percent of rice and 15.5 percent wheat yield is going to decline by 2020. In addition, it is projected that the food grain in Nepal will decrease by 5.3 percent in 2020 (MoSTE 2015). All these impacts will have major implications to the food security and well-being of majority of the population in Nepal who rely on the climate sensitive agriculture system.

Policy and Institutional Responses

At the national level, it was found that the impact of climate change and the actions needed to confront climate change have yet to be embedded into policy and planning processes (Regmi and Adhikari 2007). The agriculture ministry and its research institutions are facing huge challenges recently due to lack of human and financial resources. The government support is diverted toward other areas and less emphasis is given to agriculture sector. The research centers are almost nonfunctional due to lack of resources. This has impacted the agriculture research and innovation needed to deal with climate change issues.

The government now finally endorsed Agriculture Development Strategy (ADS). This strategy has included climate change as major threat to agriculture sector and envisioned program to address the negative consequences of climate change. However, the strategy is silent on the institutional structure and human resources needed to deliver the promises made in the strategy. Another challenge to deal with climate change in agriculture sector, both at national and local level, is related to lack of effective extension system and support services that can provide right advice to farmers and help them to overcome impact of climate change.

One of the major constraints to policy and planning in Nepal is the lack of information and knowledge on climate change (Regmi and Bhandari 2013). Although the government has developed climate stress varieties to cope with droughts and floods and few technologies, it is not tailored to local needs and priorities. Farmers are having problem in terms of taking decisions mostly during the dates for seedling, planting, weeding, fertilizer and pest management, and harvesting (Malla 2009). In specific, there is lack of concrete evidences and knowledge base to guide small holder farmers on the exact ways through which they can respond to current climate variability and future change. There are limitations to the analysis of climate change in Nepal which relies solely on the meteorological data (Shrestha and Aryal 2011). Topographic complexity over Nepal makes projecting climate changes more difficult than usual. Nepalese rainfall patterns (timing and amount) associated with the South Asian Monsoon System (SAM) are inherently complex due to highly varied topography over short distances (NCVST 2009).

Another challenge is the poor governance mechanism that is restricting the poor and vulnerable households. At present, the agriculture sector planning and budgeting process has not fully integrated climate change risks and opportunities in a comprehensive and sustained manner. As mentioned before, the national budgetary allocation for the agriculture sector is declining year by year with low investment in research and technology development. It is also evident that the agriculture extension, planning and budgeting process is not responsive to the need of poor and vulnerable communities as the policy and investment favor more rich and middle class farmers.

Framework of the Study

This study takes vulnerability first approach to understand climate change impact in agriculture sector in Nepal. Vulnerability assessment differs from traditional approaches of impact assessments in a number of important ways (Nkem et al. 2007). In essence, climate change impact assessment selects a particular environmental stress of concern and seeks to identify its most important consequences for a variety of social or ecosystem properties. The Intergovernmental Panel on Climate Change (IPCC) defined vulnerability as: "The degree to which a system is susceptible to or unable to cope with the adverse effects of climate change, including climate variability and extremes" (Brooks 2003; IPCC 2001).

Methodological Approaches

This study used from vulnerability to resilience (V2R) framework. It is a framework for analysis and action to reduce vulnerability and strengthen resilience of individuals, households, and communities. The framework sets out the key factors that contribute to peoples' vulnerability, exposure to hazards and stresses; fragile socio-economic condition and livelihoods; future risk and uncertainty; and weak governance (Practical Action 2011).

This methodology is preferred because it is suitable for analyzing community level climate vulnerability and assessing community capacity in climate change adaptation as it explores underlying causes of vulnerabilities (see Table 2.1 for detail).

In this research context, communities' vulnerability was determined by using the IPCC's guidance. This is determined qualitatively by using descriptive criteria (see Table 2.1). Vulnerability is a function of the character, magnitude, and rate of climate variation to which a system is exposed, its sensitivity, and its adaptive capacity. In other words vulnerability can be defined as a function of exposure, sensitivity, and adaptive capacity, or:

$$\text{Vulnerability} = f(\text{exposure, sensitivity, adaptive capacity})$$

where:

Exposure as defined by IPCC is "the nature and degree to which a system is exposed to significant climatic variations."

Table 2.1 The methodological approach of analyzing vulnerability of agriculture dependent communities

Vulnerability factors	Major components	Number of subcomponents
Exposure	Climate variability	Changes in temperature Changes in precipitation
	Natural disasters	Loss and damage due to natural disasters
Sensitivity	Agriculture	Food sufficiency Crop production and diversity
Adaptive capacity	Socio-economic conditions	Income status Land size Livelihood options
	Existing technology and practices	Local knowledge and practices Government support services

Source: Regmi et al. (2010).

Sensitivity as defined by IPCC is "the degree to which a system is affected, either adversely or beneficially, by climate-related stimuli."

Adaptive capacity as defined by IPCC is "the ability of a system to adjust to climate change (including climate variability and extremes), to moderate the potential damage from it, to take advantage of its opportunities, or to cope with its consequences."

Data Generation and Analysis

The research used both primary and secondary information in data gathering. The national level study focused on determining the national context of vulnerability. The study team consulted the policy makers at central level to get policy level feedback. A total of 17 policy makers and 28 practitioners involved on climate change issues were interviewed. The participants were selected purposively in order to capture the experiences and knowledge of individuals who were directly involved in policy making.

Similarly, the local level case study was conducted in Dhungegadi and Bangessal village development committees of Pyuthan district in the mid-western development region of Nepal. Altogether 128 communities were directly interviewed using semi-structured interview.

Similarly, a total of nine focus group discussions were carried out with communities and local stakeholders in the selected villages including key informant interview with seven individuals and informal interactions. The participants for the interview at household level were selected randomly by using stratified random sampling. Stratified random sampling was used to best represent the ethnic group, sex, and different categories of household. Likewise, the participants for group discussion and key informant interview were selected purposively in order to involve different category of households and interested and knowledgeable individuals.

The data gathering used the participatory tools and techniques to enrich the information generation and discussion. The primary information was collected through in-depth interviews with key stakeholders as well as focus group discussions with representative from the farmers and members of forest user group, taking gender, age, social position, and income into account. Participatory tools included vulnerability mapping, field observation, and focus group discussion.

General Description of the Study Areas

About the Study Site

The case study was conducted in Bangesaal and Dhungegadi VDCs of Pyuthan district of Nepal. These two VDCs were selected for the study because of their relevance to generate local level learning. These two VDCs are also among the pioneer VDCs to be involved in climate change adaptation planning in Nepal. Pyuthan is a hilly district that lies in Rapti zone of mid-western region of Nepal. It lies within the latitudes 27°55′ to 28°25′ N and longitudes 82°30′ to 83°0′ E (see Figure 2.1). The total area of the district is 1,309 square km with the altitude ranging from 305 m asl (above sea level) to 3,659 m asl. Due to this wide variation in altitude, climate ranges from tropical to temperate. Three major rivers, Mandavi (Madi), Rapti, and Jhimruk, provide importance source of income and livelihoods support for the district because it generates electricity, provides irrigation and drinking water support. The average maximum temperature of the district is 23.3°C and minimum is 14.8°C with the annual precipitation of 1,294.5 ml (DDC Pyuthan 2008).

Figure 2.1 Map showing the study area

Source: By Regmi and Paudya

The two study sites, Dhungegadi and Bangesaal VDCs, lie in the southern region of the Pyuthan district. The study sites are adjoining VDCs sharing common socio-economic features. These VDCs are located in the basement of Churiya region[1] of Nepal. Both the VDCs are rich in natural resources mostly forest and water resources. The land and ecological condition of the VDCs are slightly different. Dhungegadi VDC has most of the settlement in the hilly terrain while Bangesaal VDCs settlement is in the plain. The secondary information shows that Bangesaal VDC has a total of 3,325.60 hectares of forest land and more than three dozens of small river ponds and lakes (DDC Pyuthan 2008).

Communities Are Highly Exposed to Climate Risk in the Study Areas

This section of the findings argues that climate change is happening very rapidly in Nepal. Climate change is assessed, in this chapter, based on the analysis of variability in temperature and rainfall (Shrestha et al. 1999, 2000). The national scenarios of climate change vulnerability show that,

---

[1] The Churia region (or area) consists of the Terai and the Siwalik range physiographic units. The Churia hills are geologically young and fragile and consist of about 26.6 percent of the total area of Nepal.

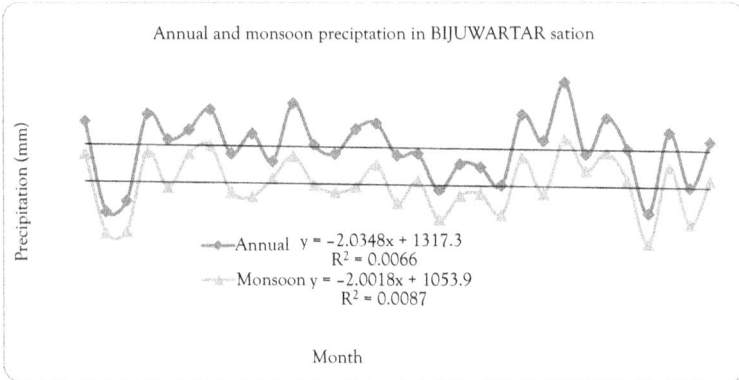

Annual and monsoon preciptation in BIJUWARTAR sation

Precipitation (mm)

——Annual y = –2.0348x + 1317.3
                    R² = 0.0066
—·— Monsoon y = –2.0018x + 1053.9
                        R² = 0.0087

Month

Figure 2.2 Annual and monsoon rainfall trend in Bijuwartar station

Source: By Regmi and Paudya

among the geographic ranking of districts, Pyuthan (the study district) falls in medium category (MoE 2010). The analysis of precipitation data (from 1975 to 2003) of the station in Pyuthan district (Bijuwartar[2]) shows that the average rainfall has slightly changed (see Figure 2.2). The analysis shows an overall decreasing precipitation trend by 2.03 mm per annum. The monsoon participation between the same time periods also shows a decreasing trend by 2.0 mm per year. This decreasing trend is however not that significant (see Figure 2.2). Similar analysis on precipitation data, at the national level, also does not reveal any significant trends (Shrestha and Aryal 2011).

The analysis of 30 years of temperature data of the nearest station that is, Dang Deukhuri station[3] shows that temperature is increasing. The mean annual maximum temperature trend from 1975 to 2005 in study area has increased. The mean annual maximum temperature is increasing at rate of 0.055°C. This increasing trend is slightly higher than the national mean temperature increase which is 0.04°C per year (Baidya, Shrestha, and Sheikh 2008). The rate of increase is even higher at five years interval which is 0.06°C per year. Analysis of the trend of

---

[2] The station is located at an altitude of 823 m above sea level.
[3] This station is at 725 msl and similar to the two study VDCs. This station data was used because of the lack of meteorological data within the study district.

temperature increase shows that temperature will significantly increase in years to come if the GHGs will not be stabilized in the atmosphere. Among many, the report produced by NCVST (2009) shows greater climatic variability and increase in temperature over the country with rise from 0.5 to 2°C with a multi-model mean of 1.4°C by the 2030s.

Result and Findings

Climate Change Is Aggravating the Increase in Disaster Risk and Impact

This section of the chapter argues that with the increase in temperature and variability in rainfall, the disaster risk and impact has been increasing in the study areas. The field level information showed that the trend of occurrence of climate-induced disasters has increased in recent years. All the respondents (n = 128) perceived that there is increased trend of disaster occurrence in their locality. They have named flood, landslide, fire, and draught as the major disasters affecting them. The government data of Pyuthan district shows that the trend of disaster frequency has increased in recent years with the number of casualties and property loss (MoHA 2009).

The casualties of climate-induced disaster (flood and landslide) has taken lives of rural people and devastated their livelihoods. The trend of disaster frequency has increased in recent years with the number of casualties and property loss (MoHA 2009). The vulnerability assessment carried out in the Dhungegadi by the Livelihoods and Forestry Program of Pyuthan district showed that more than 200 households (out of 753) were directly impacted from fire, draught, and landslide problems in between 1999 and 2009. In Bangessal VDC of Pyuthan, in Ward Number 5, the outbreak of water-borne diseases (cholera and diarrhea) in 2008–2009 took life of two villagers. It happened during extreme flooding season (Rupantaran 2012). The historical timeline reported in Local Adaptation Plan of Action (LAPA)[4], prepared at Dhungegadi, also shows that the impact of disasters in communities' livelihood is massive (refer to

---

[4] It is adaptation plan prepared by communities at the local level.

Table 2.2 The historical time line analysis of disaster trend in Dhungegadi (2007–2010)

Year	Major climate disasters	Impact on communities
2010	Draught, landslide, outbreak of diseases, extreme wind	One dead due to diarrhea, a total of 46 household affected
		Loss of 11 livestock due to outbreak of disease
2009	Disease in paddy, draught, landslide, and extreme wind	Loss of agriculture land and production decline, a total of 5 household impacted
		69 livestock dead due to disease outbreak of 20 poor families
		Fire outbreak damaged 13 houses
2008	Draught, fire outbreak, diseases in livestock, landslide and hailstone	11 household directly impacted due to drying of local water sources
		Damage of agriculture land
		Fire damaged 6 houses
2007	Draught, fire outbreak, diseases in livestock	Due to drying of local spring 57 ropani* of land was left barren
		18 houses were destroyed due to fire outbreak
		150 livestock dead due to disease outbreak
		Wheat production declined due to lack of water

Source: Focus group discussion with communities in the research sites February, 2012 (by the researchers)

*1 hectare = 19.8 ropani.

Table 2.2). The result implies that with increased climate change disasters, the livelihood losses will be extremely high and costly.

Impact of Climate Change on Agriculture and Rural Well-being

This section of the chapter examines how climate change is posing threat to the agriculture system and impacting the rural livelihoods. Extreme events will have greater impacts on sectors with closer links to climate, such as water, agriculture and food security, forestry, health, and tourism (Field et al. 2012). The household survey also indicated the strong perception of communities toward impact of climate change in agriculture. The following section outlines the implication of climate change in agriculture system of the study sites.

Agriculture is the major occupation in rural areas. In the two study sites (Dhungegadi and Bangesaal of Pyuthan district) more than 62 percent of the households directly rely on agriculture for their livelihood. Communities strongly perceived that the impact of climate change was higher in Dhungegadi and Bangesaal VDC. All the respondents in two village development committees felt that climate change will have impact on agriculture. There was no response on the low impact side which suggests the strong feeling on impact of climate change on agriculture. The respondent's issues in terms of production were concentrated around decline of production and yield of major cereal and cash crops. They have pointed out the lack of rainfall as major obstacle to the declining productivity.

In focus group discussion, communities of Bangesaal VDC mentioned that in 1999, they were forced to leave their land barren because they were not prepared for draught that year. The delay in monsoon season had major impact on the rain fed agriculture system where majority of farmers have to rely on monsoon rain for cultivation. Farmers experienced production decline of some cash crops (pea, gram, lentil, turmeric, mustard). There was also sharp decline of production of maize, wheat, mustard, potato, and so on. Out of 128 respondents, 37 felt that production decline was the major impact of climate change in agriculture. Respondents also reported that the expansion of invasive species threatened the production of major stable crops.

The loss of major agriculture crops has been an issue in the study sites. The farmers in the study area have mentioned that the traditional landraces of rice like *Simtharo, Marsi, Hasi* have been lost due to rainfall variability. According to the farmers, these local varieties need continuous rainfall for four months in order to mature and yield. In absence of ideal climatic condition, majority of the local species could not yield high and thus farmers were forced to abandon. There are other studies in Nepal which have stated that climate change is one of the major causes of loss of local crops (Regmi et al. 2009; Manandhar et al. 2011).

The findings show that there are various factors that contributed in declining agriculture productivity in the area. During focus group discussion with communities in Bangesaal it was revealed that the main cause of declining agriculture productivity is due to rainfall variability, low input, loss of soil fertility, labor shortages, and outbreak of pest and diseases. Among the five major factors that contributed in lower agriculture production, three were reported to be linked directly to climate change variables such as temperature and rainfall. While low agriculture input and labor shortages are socio-economic factors that also contributed in decreasing agriculture productivity. This finding implies that climate change is adding to the existing problem and making it more complex. Likewise, it suggests that climate change impact should not be examined in isolation but has to be assessed within the existing socio-economic scenarios at the local level.

Climate change Is a Major Threat to Food Security

This section of the chapter argues that climate change has worsened the food security situation in the study site. The survey data in the study sites shows that average food sufficiency status is 7.2 months. This means with the existing produce from the land, the household can feed their family for almost seven months. The data further reveal that only 21 percent have food sufficiency[5] while the rest 79 percent have to struggle. There is not much different in the food sufficiency status between two of the VDCs. However, in case of Dhungegadi VDC the data generated from household survey show in average one month less food sufficiency compared to the VDC profile of the government prepared in 2009 which shows average food sufficiency of eight months per year. The government VDC survey data also shows that 28.4 percent of the total population has sufficient food for the whole year (DDC Pyuthan 2008).

The production of agriculture crops has direct linkages with the food security situation. During survey, majority of the households revealed that the food sufficient status of household is decreasing. During focus group discussion, the farmers said that they used to have 12-month food sufficiency 10 years back and now they have only 6 to 7 months. Although there might be various other reasons, mostly the interviewed farmers have identified climate variability as the major cause. For example, the farmers

[5] The VDC data of Bangesaal also show that only 22 percent have food sufficiency while the rest have to struggle.

have said that the production of agriculture crops have gone down due to changes in monsoon pattern. According to them, the unpredictability of the monsoon has influenced their cropping pattern. For example, the communities of Bangesaal revealed that they suffered from the loss of paddy transplanting material in 2009 due to delay in monsoon.

The impact of climate-related disasters on the agriculture land and assets is also having impact on food security. The land holding size is in an average of 12.7 ropani with household having minimum of 1 ropani (1 hectare = 19.965 ropani) to household with maximum of 65 ropani. There are only 16.4 percent of households who have more than 1–2 hectare of agriculture land and only 3.9 percent have more than 2 hectares of land. The national data also show that 50 percent of the population have only 0.5 hectare of land and other 4 percent have 2 ha and more land (CBS 2011). The limited land holding size has made the poor household more at risk and vulnerable. There were other studies carried out in Nepal which show that climate change is having negative impact on food security in the rural areas of Nepal mostly due to production decline (Grist 2015; Shrestha and Nepal 2016).

Sensitivity of Population to Climate Change

Poor Socio-Economic Conditions in the Site

This section of the chapter argues that besides, physical risk, the socio-economic condition also influences vulnerability of households to climate change. The census data show that agriculture is the major source of income in both Dhungegadi and Bangesaal VDCs. Majority of the population depend on agriculture activities to sustain their livelihood (CBS 2011). The district profile also shows that more than 70 percent of the population depends on agriculture (DDC Pyuthan 2008). Therefore, dependency of communities on climate sensitive sector like agriculture makes them more vulnerable.

Although labor migration has been good for rural economy, the rural agriculture in Nepal has suffered. The socio-economic data show that the migration trend in the VDCs is higher. The survey result shows that 56.3 percent of the respondents have indicated that some of their family members have migrated to either to national cities or abroad for work. The secondary data also show that among the migrants, majority are male. The government data of Bangesaal VDC taken in 2009 also shows that out of total migrant population 98.8 percent are male (VDC Profile Bangesaal 2009).

Majority of the participants, during focus group discussion, stated that migration has resulted in the shortage of labor for agriculture farming and hence contributed in decreasing agriculture productivity (FGDC February, 2012). The vast amount of land in the hilly areas of Nepal, as in case of the study areas, are suffering from the trend of leaving uncultivated and barren land. The cultivation land in the study areas is difficult and labor intensive. As male migrate abroad for work, the female household have to take full responsibility of cultivation. This has increased the work burden of female households and thus left no other option for them than leaving the land barren. Likewise, it was revealed that young people have migrated more compared to aged ones.

The findings show that migration has not improved the food security situation of the poor households. The household survey shows that 31.3 percent of the income source is from agriculture, 9.4 percent from remittances and 25 percent from both remittances and agriculture. In case of poor household, more than 10 percent of the income is from remittances. However, majority of the interviewed household argue that it has not substantially contributed in food security as they still cannot afford to purchase land or do investment in the farm. In summary, the demographic and socio-economic condition of the study site reveals that majority of the population in the study area are dependent on subsistence-based agriculture with hardly enough produce to feed their large family size (the average family size is 6.7). There are similarities in the two VDCs surveyed in terms of socio-economic features. The outcome of survey indicates that there are issues of literacy (the survey shows that more than 50 percent of the respondents do not have access to education), food sufficiency, labor, and physical and financial assets. More than 50 percent of the population in the study site are below poverty line and have limited opportunities because of their limited access to agriculture land and education status. Only 5 percent of the population has sufficient land, sufficient food to eat, and good income.

Socio-Cultural Barriers to Climate Change Adaptation

The previous section clearly showed the poor livelihood scenarios of the households. This section provides evidences to support the fact that socio-cultural barriers contribute to increase vulnerability at the local level. The group discussion revealed that the household which had limited land with higher dependency on agriculture and other common pool resource like water were comparatively vulnerable than household with more land and other alternative economic activities. There were examples in the Bangesaal village when the flooding washed way agriculture land, it was the household with limited land with no other alternative business who were almost landless and food insecure than the household who had other land and alternative. It was revealed that the limited land made poor more susceptible and vulnerable to the impacts of climate extremes (Outcome of FGD with communities January, 2012).

The impact of climate change is higher among poor, women, and ethnic minorities due to their limited assets, financial resources, and nature of livelihood (Mainlay and Tan 2012) Compared to other resources like agriculture and forest, agriculture land is mostly common resources where poor household depend on for their livelihood. One of the female respondent shares story about the devastation and impact of flooding from three small rivers. Part of her house and all the agriculture land was washed way. She also lost her livestock during that flooding. She had to rescue her children and had to stay in neighbors' house. Likewise, during focus group discussion also the participants shared that more than 70 percent of the victims of flooding and landslide are poor households. For example, in Ward Number 5 of Bangesaal, the outbreak of water-borne diseases (Cholera and diarrhea) in 2008-2009 took life of two people belonging to poor families. It happened during extreme flooding season. People had to drink the dirty water and the outbreak happened.

Similarly, women who were more responsible to the household activities were more vulnerable than their male counterparts. The women faced challenges to arrange food, fetch water, and satisfy their family needs. Due to negative impact of climate variability on agriculture and water resources, women had to travel far distance or spend time queuing for water collection. The comparison of data generated from the focus group discussion and secondary sources indicates that in between 2009 and 2012, there have been drastic changes in the local water availability context. In recent years, 42 percent of the women have to travel more than 30 min to collect water compared to only 23 percent in 2009.[6]

It was found that the work in agriculture land was labor intensive and less productive compared to the past. The female respondents in the interview revealed that due to climate extremes, more input is needed in agriculture. According to them, the agriculture production system has become more difficult and costly nowadays compared to 10 years ago. In addition, the male migration also has added in the work pressure for women and other members of the family. The labor shortages have added additional burden for women to explore food and resources to sustain their living.

The impact of climate change was reported higher among ethnic and disadvantaged group due to their lack of access to education (information and knowledge) and other resources (finance and technology). Comparatively, the poor, marginalized, and disadvantaged groups were more impacted due to their limited assets, financial resources, and nature of livelihood (more dependent). In the interview one of the key informants from Bangesaal provides example of how mostly poor household suffer from climate change impacts compared to the rich one. According to him, in Atitaar and Allenephant, 75 poor and vulnerable household belonging to disadvantaged group have been impacted.

The findings also show that socio-cultural context in the study site impacted people's ability to respond effectively to climate risk and impact. One of the female respondents from marginalized ethnic group added by saying "the problem is severe within the poor household and communities like mine. We are treated as second-class citizen because we are not involved in community level decision making in terms of prioritizing development and mobilizing resources." During the focus group discussion, it was further revealed that the poor and vulnerable households are dependent on the higher castes, elites, and powerful individuals within the community groups for receiving benefits from the projects or

---

[6] Outcome of Focus group discussion in Dhungegadi VDC.

programs. This developed due to the deep-routed culture at the local level that constrained participation and access to benefits for the poor, women, and other disadvantaged groups.

Adaptive Capacity of Communities

This section of the chapter discusses on the existing capacity of households to respond to climate change impacts. In contrary to the degree of exposure and sensitivity, the adaptive capacity of communities is lower. There are local level practices, like soil and water management and organic farming, to cope with climate extremes. These local practices are based on local knowledge generated from experiences and practices of communities over generations. The interview with communities in Dhungegadi and Bangesaal showed that there are some traditional practices to cope with climate change impacts practiced. Majority of respondents in both VDCs felt that they have adopted traditional practices to deal with climate change impacts. The perception on existence of traditional practices, like use of low cost agriculture practices, is higher in Dhungegadi (62.5 percent) compared to Bangesaal (54.5 percent). There was also higher number of respondents who did not adopt any kind of traditional practices. According to the non-adopters, they didn't adapt because they were not aware about the suitable technology that works better in the extreme situations.

At the research sites, the traditional practices adapted at the household level were mostly related to efficient water management, plantation, and local bioengineering practices. Around 23 percent of the respondents used kitchen waste for irrigating their vegetable crops. Communities also practiced plantation and bioengineering practices to protect the land from landslide and flooding. Some adopted the local irrigation practices to reduce the risk and impact of climate. There were also other national level studies which document local knowledge in relation to climate change. These studies have provided examples of some of the practices adapted by communities and indicated the limitations to deal with climate extremes.

There are limits to local knowledge and strategies adapted by communities to deal with climate extremes (Regmi and Bhandari 2013). Findings of the household survey during the research also support the above outcome of researchers around limitation of traditional adaptation practices.

The analysis of household responses indicates that even with households adopting the traditional practices, the impact of climate change is high. Almost 89.1 percent of the respondents in both the VDCs perceived that the existing adaptation options were ineffective and could not address the climate risk and impact. Only around 11 percent of the respondents felt that the traditional practices are effective to deal with some of the disasters and not all. The effectiveness differed in household responses because of the factor governing the type of technology and experiences of its impact. Half of the respondents (64) perceived that the traditional practices were ineffective because of the lack of information, knowledge, and technology.

The problem exists in terms of availability of location-specific climate-relevant information, provision of agro-advisories, and access of small holder farmers to weather-based agro-advisory information and services that is suitable for making decisions on agriculture practices. During the focus group discussion in Dhungegadi and Bangesaal VDCs, more than 90 percent of farmers mentioned that they do not have access to weather data and weather-based agriculture guidance in order to respond to the issues such as climate change. The first issue mentioned by majority of farmers (82 percent) is the lack of weather data suitable for agriculture decision making. More than 76 percent of respondents also mentioned that there is lack of weather-based agro-advisories at local level that can address location-specific issues of small holder farmers. During focus group discussion in Dhungegadi, farmers mentioned that there is lack of effective communication mechanism that can facilitate the sharing of information among scientists, extension agents, private sector, and farmers.

The above discussions clearly imply that there are issues in responding to climate change effectively at the local level. The forced field analysis[7] carried out during focus group discussions in Dhungegadi VDC, among the communities, also showed critical gap in terms of responding

---

[7] This is one of the PRA tools to rank communities' perception on the comparative assessment of severity of problem versus the effectiveness of existing practices. It is ranked using the scale of 1–5 (low-high). The existing practices were related to technology and practices adopted by communities and the input from government and nongovernmental sectors.

to climate change given the severity of the disasters. According to FGD (focused group discussion) community members Dhungegadi (2012), the draught and landslide were among the top disasters (scoring the highest 5 in terms of severity of issue) but the existing practices to cope were less effective (scoring only 2). This shows a critical gap in terms of existing capacity of communities to address the severity of climate change disasters. Similar exercise was carried out in Bangesaal VDC and the result also shows that the existing and available knowledge and practices are in sufficient to address the impact of climate-induced disasters.

The major capacity issues identified at the local level include: (a) lack of access to information, knowledge, and technology on dealing with climate risk and impact; (b) lack of access to financial services such as climate risk financing; (c) lack of support from the government and other agencies; (d) existing income gaps and lack of opportunities; (e) weak local governance mostly related to low capacity of local institutions, limited awareness among communities and disparity in resource use. The respondents during interview also shared that the current government extension support in agriculture sector is inadequate and mostly lack technical skills in terms of addressing emerging issues like climate change. The agriculture officers interviewed also realized that they have inadequate technical skills and knowledge to deal with new issues and problems in the agriculture sector.

There are studies which show that if communities' degree of exposure and sensitivity is higher and the adaptive capacity of communities is lower, then they are vulnerable to climate change (Smit and Pilifosova 2003; Cannon and Mahn-Muller 2010). The information in the two VDCs, studied in this research, also shows that the risk and exposure of communities is higher because agriculture sector is more impacted by climate change. On the contrary, adaptive capacity of communities in the study area is low due to extreme poverty, weak governance structure, and limited access to technological and financial resources.

Discussion and Implications

The findings showed that poor socio-economic condition of household is one of the major factors for increased climate risk and vulnerability.

Among the population, the women and poor households were most vulnerable due to their exposure, limited socio-economic capability, and complex socio-structural context to respond to climate change impact. This is because impact of climate change was hitting hard the populations, the households who were mostly dependent on the sensitive resources and do not have any alternative. The local knowledge and practices on dealing with climate disaster were observed but mostly ineffective due to limited access to external knowledge and technologies. The findings also show that climate change had emerged as an additional burden piled up to the existing problem of socio-economic backwardness, in equality and lack of access to better services.

This means we have to consider adaptation and development together in order to address both poverty and vulnerability. It also implies that standalone climate change adaptation interventions will not be able to address the root cause of vulnerability. The findings also imply that it is necessary that climate change adaptation is mainstreamed with other development policies and plans. In order to counter this problem, pre-emptive action and reform is required within the agricultural sector to better respond to issues of food security and degrading agriculture economy caused by climate change and other socio-economic turmoil.

The above research findings suggest that just fixing the climate risk is not going to address the root cause of climate change. The intrinsic link between risk and hazard with socio-structural context of communities has been evident in this research. This implies that vulnerability reduction and sustainable development agenda has to be thought in an integrated manner and complementary to each other to address agriculture and food security issue. There are other findings which also demonstrate the strong linkages of development factors and climate change vulnerability. Schipper (2007) argues that vulnerability reduction and sustainable development as fundamental elements of adaptation to climate change.

Similarly, the findings suggest that local responses in agriculture sector alone are not sufficient enough to address the food security issues. The local and community level response measure is often undermined and complicated by lack of weather-related information, knowledge, and technological barriers at local level. It shows the complicated nature of vulnerability. Furthermore, Yamin, Rahman, and Huq (2005) also argue

CLIMATE CHANGE ON AGRICULTURE AND FOOD SECURITY   39

that complexities of climate change problem necessitate addressing the *structural* causes of vulnerability that cannot be addressed in a piecemeal, project-by-project fashion.

The findings imply that local responses have to be supported with technology transfer, risk-based financing mechanisms, and knowledge and skills to deal with climate extremes. In specific, there is a need to tailor weather-based agriculture information and advisories to suit household and communities in need. Adger, Arnell, and Tompkins (2005) argue that reliable climate and weather information provides farmers with knowledge about dealing with farm level uncertainty and risk. This could be achieved if we link communities with scientist and policy makers and adapt a more integrated approach of reducing risk and addressing multiple drivers of vulnerability, so that role of multiple agencies and actors will be relevant.

The findings further suggest that reducing vulnerability in agriculture sector in Nepal can be the entry point of adaptation in agriculture sector. However, we must keep in mind that the overemphasis on the vulnerability context also undermines the specific risk and hazards' severity and impact. Besides climate risk and sensitivity, the findings suggest that vulnerability in agriculture sector in Nepal is influenced by multiple factors that are related to socio-structural context, governance structure, and political economy of the area. The complexity in determining the vulnerability context of communities often makes the intervention and prioritization very difficult. According to Canon and Mahn (2010) and Ayers (2011), vulnerability looks a problem-solving-oriented approach so may lead to short-term and projectized interventions. This outlines the need for carrying out more research to answer some of the complexities associated with vulnerability and finding the right means for intervention.

Conclusion

The information in this chapter demonstrates the intrinsic link between the socio-economic context and impact of climate change on agriculture in Nepal. The information shows that besides physical risk, the socio-economic, cultural, and development and political context also shaped country's exposure to risk and vulnerability to agriculture and food security. Information described in the chapter also show that it's the poor who are suffering from both development deficit situations and impacts of climate risk. The commonality in the population at risk and exposure often supports the argument for bringing climate change and agriculture development together.

Agriculture and food security is going to be impacted severely by climate change. The existing capacity at the local and national level is low. The existing national and local level efforts are inadequate to deal with climate change. Existing system severely lacks political will, knowledge base, and institutional and financial mechanism to deal with urgency of climate change. Due to high exposure and sensitivity and limited capacity, the large number of rural population in the study areas are vulnerable to the impact of climate change in agriculture and food security.

This means the national government has to develop strategy to fill the knowledge, technology, and financial gap in terms of urgently dealing with climate change. The complexity of climate change, as argued earlier, thus demands the working collaboration among international, national, and local actors. It further demands innovative approaches and systems that ensure sustainable knowledge flow and communication mechanisms between scientists, intermediaries, and farmers and necessary supports to the farmers. Nepal has the opportunities to address the current constraints in agriculture sector in responding to climate change by integrating climate change in the national and sectoral planning processes which can be done by reflecting in the National Adaptation Plan (NAP) process and mainstreaming climate change in ADS and other relevant policies.

References

Adger, W., N. Arnell, and E. Tompkins. 2005. "Successful Adaptation to Climate Change across Scales." *Global Environmental Change* 15, no. 2, pp. 77–86.
Alam, M., and B.R. Regmi. 2004. "Adverse Impacts of Climate Change on Development of Nepal: Integrating Adaptation into Policies and Activities." CLACC Working Paper. Dhaka: Bangladesh Centre for Advanced Studies (BCAS).

Ayers, J. 2011. "Resolving the Adaptation Paradox: Exploring the Potential for Deliberative Adaptation Policy-Making in Bangladesh." *Global Environmental Politics* 11, no. 1, pp. 62–88.

Baidya, S., M. Shrestha, and M.M. Sheikh. 2008. "Trends in Daily Climatic Extremes of Temperature and Precipitation in Nepal." *Journal of Hydrology and Meteorology* 5, no. 1, pp. 38–53.

Biggs, E.M., E.L. Tompkins, J. Allen, C. Moon, and R. Allen. 2013. "Agricultural Adaptation to Climate Change: Observations from the Mid-Hills of Nepal." *Climate and Development* 5, no. 2, pp. 165–73.

Brooks, N. 2003. "Vulnerability, Risk and Adaptation: A Conceptual Framework." *Tyndall Centre for Climate Change Research Working Paper* 38, pp. 1–16.

Cannon, T., and D. Mahn-Muller. 2010. "Vulnerability, Resilience and Development Discourses in Context of Climate Change." *Natural Hazards* 55, no. 3, p. 621.

CBS 2011. *Preliminary Findings of the National Census 2011.* Kathmandu, Nepal: Centre Bureau of Statistics.

Chaudhury, A.S., M.J. Ventresca, T.F. Thornton, A. Helfgott, C. Sova, P. Baral, and J. Ligthart. 2016. "Emerging Meta-organizations and Adaptation to Global Climate Change: Evidence from Implementing Adaptation in Nepal, Pakistan and Ghana." *Global Environmental Change* 38, pp. 243–57.

DDC Pyuthan 2008. *DDC Profile Report.* Pyuthan: District Development Committee, Ministry of Local Development.

Field, C.B., V. Barros, T.F. Stocker, Q. Dahe, D.J. Dokken, K.L. Ebi, M.D. Mastrandrea, K.J. Mach, G. K. Plattner, S.K. Allen, M. Tignor and P.M. Midgley. 2012. *Managing the Risks of Extreme Events and Disasters to Advance Climate Change Adaptation: Special Report of the Intergovernmental Panel on Climate Change.* London: Cambridge University Press.

Gentle, P., and T.N. Maraseni. 2012. "Climate Change, Poverty and Livelihoods: Adaptation Practices by Rural Mountain Communities in Nepal." *Environmental Science & Policy* 21, pp. 24–34.

Grist, N. 2015. Nepal's Agriculture, Climate Change and Food Security: Country Analysis and Programming Recommendations, viii. Evidence on Demand, UK.

Hijioka, Y., E. Lin, J.J. Pereira, R.T. Corlett, X. Cui, G.E. Insarov, R.D. Lasco, E. Lindgren, and A. Surjan. 2014. *Climate Change 2014: Impacts, Adaptation, and Vulnerability. Part B: Regional Aspects. Contribution of Working Group II to the Fifth Assessment Report of the Intergovernmental Panel on Climate Change*— Asia. In eds. V.R. Barros, C.B. Field, D.J. Dokken, M.D. Mastrandrea, K.J. Mach, T.E. Bilir, M. Chatterjee, K.L. Ebi, Y.O. Estrada, R.C. Genova, B. Girma, E.S. Kissel, A.N. Levy, S. MacCracken, P.R. Mastrandrea, and L.L. White, 1327–70. Cambridge, United Kingdom and New York: Cambridge University Press.

Intergrated Development Society Nepal (IDS-Nepal), Practical Action (PA) and Global Climate Adaptation Partnership (GCCA). 2014. *Economic Impact Assessment of Climate Change in Key Sectors in Nepal.* Kathmandu, Nepal: IDS-Nepal.

IPCC 2001. *Climate Change 2001: The Scientific Basis. Contribution of Working Group I to the Third Assessment Report of the Intergovernmental Panel on Climate Change.* In eds. J.T. Houghton, Y. Ding, D.J. Griggs, M. Noguer, P.J. van der Linden, X. Dai, K. Maskell, and C.A. Johnson. Cambridge, United Kingdom and New York USA: Cambridge University Press.

IPCC 2014. Impacts, Adaptation, and Vulnerability. Contribution of Working Group II to the Fifth Assessment Report of the Intergovernmental Panel on Climate Change. Retrieved from IPCC website http://ipccwg2.gov

Knox, J., T. Hess, A. Daccache, and Y. Wheeler. 2012. "Climate Change Impacts on Crop Productivity in Africa and South Asia." *Environmental Research Letters* 7, no. 3, 1–8. doi:10.1088/1748-9326/7/3/034032

Mainlay, J., and S.F. Tan. 2012. *Mainstreaming Gender and Climate Change in Nepal.* In eds. S. Fisher and H. Reid, 1–16. London: International Institute for Environment and Development (IIED).

Malla, G. 2009. "Climate Change and its Impact on Nepalese Agriculture." *Journal of Agriculture and Environment* 9, pp. 62–71.

Manandhar, S., D. Vogt, P.R. Sylvain, and K. Futuba. 2011. "Adapting Cropping Systems to Climate Change in Nepal: a Cross-Regional Study of Farmers' Perception and Practices." *Regional Environmental Change* 11, no. 2, pp. 335–48.

Ministry of Environment (MoE). 2010. *National Adaptation Programme of Action.* Kathmandu, Nepal: Ministry of Environment.

Ministry of Home Affairs (MOHA). 2009. *Nepal Disaster Report 2009.* Kathmandu: Ministry of Home Affairs-Nepal.

Ministry of Science, Technology and Environment (MoSTE). 2015. *Third National Communication Report to UNFCCC. Unpublished.* Kathmandu: MoSTE, Nepal.

Nepal Climate Vulnerability Study Team (NCVST). 2009. *Vulnerability Through the Eyes of Vulnerable: Climate Change Induced Uncertainties and Nepal's Development Predicaments.* Kathmandu: ISET.

Nkem, J., H. Santoso, M. Daniel, B. Maria, and K. Markku. 2007. "Using Tropical Forest Ecosystem Goods and Services for Planning Climate Change Adaptation with Implications for Food Security and Poverty Reduction." *SAT eJournal* 4, no. 1, pp. 1–23.

Oxfam 2009. *Even The Himalayas Has Stopped Similing: Climate Change, Poverty and Adaptation in Nepal. Report Summary.* Kathmandu: Oxfam international-Nepal office.

Poudel, S., and K. Kotani. 2012. "Climatic Impacts on Crop Yield and its Variability in Nepal: Do they Vary Across Seasons and Altitudes?" *Climatic Change* 116, no. 2, pp. 327–55.

Practical Action 2009. *Temporal and Spatial Variability of Climate Change over Nepal (1976-2005).* Kathmandu: Practical Action.

Practical Action 2011. *From Vulnerability to Resilience: A framework for analysis and action to build community Resilience*, In ed. K. Pasteur. United Kingdom: Practical Action Publishing.

Regmi, B.R., and A. Adhikari. 2007. "Climate Change and Human Development-Risk and Vulnerability in a Warming World (HDR 2007 Nepal Case Study), Occassional Paper." Human Development Report Office, HDR 2007, UNDP.

Regmi, B.R., L. Thapa, R. Suwal, S. Khadka, G.B. Sharma, and B.B. Tamang. 2009. "Agro-biodiversity Management: An Opportunity for Mainstreaming Community-based Adaptation to Climate Change." *Journal of Forest and Livelihood* 8, no. 1, pp. 113–21.

Regmi, B., A. Morcrette, A. Paudyal, R. Bastakoti, and A. Pradhan. 2010. *Participatory Tools and Techniques for Assessing Climate Change Impacts and Exploring Adaptation Option. A Community Based Tool Kit for Practitioners.* Kathmandu: Livelihoods and Forestry Program (LFP)/UK Aid.

Regmi, B., and D. Bhandari. 2013. "Climate Change Adaptation in Nepal: Exploring Ways to Overcome the Barriers." *Journal of Forest and Livelihood* 11, no. 1, pp. 43–61.

Rupantaran, N. 2012. *Climate Change Vulnerability Mapping for Pyuthan District.* Kathmandu: Rupantaran Nepal.

Sapkota, S., M.N. Paudel, N.S. Thakur, M.B. Nepali, and R. Neupane. 2011. "Effect of Climate Change on Rice Production: A Case of Six VDCs in Jumla District." *Nepal Journal of Science and Technology* 11, pp. 57–62.

Schipper, E.L.F. 2007. "Climate Change Adaptation and Development: Exploring the Linkages." Tyndall Centre Working Paper. UK: Tyndall Centre for Climate Change Research.

Shrestha, A.B., C.P. Wake, P.A. Mayewski, and J.E. Dibb. 1999. "Maximum Temperature Trends in the Himalaya and its Vicinity: An Analysis Based on Temperature Records from Nepal for the period 1971–94." *Journal of Climate* 12, no. 9, pp. 2775–86.

Shrestha, A.B., C.P. Wake, P.A. Mayewski, and J.E. Dibb. 2000. "Precipitation Fluctuations in the Nepal Himalaya and its Vicinity and Relationship with Some Large Scale Climatological Parameters." *International Journal of Climatology* 20, no. 3, pp. 317–27.

Shrestha, A.B., and R. Aryal. 2011. "Climate Change in Nepal and its Impact on Himalayan Glaciers." *Regional Environmental Change* 11, no. 1, pp. 65–77.

Shrestha, R.P., and N. Nepal. 2016. "An Assessment by Subsistence Farmers of the Risks to Food Security Attributable to Climate Change in Makwanpur, Nepal." *Food Security* 8, no. 2, pp. 415–25.

Smit, B., and O. Pilifosova. 2003. "From Adaptation to Adaptive Capacity and Vulnerability Reduction Climate Change." In *Adaptive Capacity and Development,* eds. R.J.T. Klein, S.Huq and J.B. Smith*,* 9–28. London: Imperial College Press.

VDC Profile 2009. *Village Development Profile of Dhungegadi VDC-Pyuthan District.* Pyuthan: District Development Committee.

Vermeulen, S.J., B.M. Campbell, and J.S.I. Ingram. 2012. "Climate Change and Food Systems." *Environment and Resources* 37, pp. 195–222.

World Food Programme (WFP). 2009. *Food security Situation in Nepal.* Kathmandu, Nepal: WFP.

Yamin, F., A. Rahman, and S. Huq. 2005. "Vulnerability, Adaptation and Climate Disasters: A Conceptual Overview." *IDS Bulletin* 36, no. 4, p. 1.

Further Reading

Food and Agriculture Organization of the United Nations. 2008. *Climate Change and Food Security: A Framework Document.* Rome: Food and Agriculture Organization of the United Nations.

Lal, R., M.V.K. Sivakumar, M.A. Faiz, A.H.M. Mustafizur Rahman, and K.R. Islam. (Eds.). 2011. *Climate Change and Food Security in South Asia.* Netherlands: Springer.

Moorhead, A. 2009. *Climate, Agriculture and Food Security: A Strategy for Change.* Montpellier, Cedex: Alliance of the CGIAR Centers.

Zewdie, A. 2014. "Impacts of Climate Change on Food Security: A Literature Review in Sub Saharan Africa." *Journal of Earth Science and Climate Change* 5, 225. doi:10.4172/2157-7617.1000225

CHAPTER 3

Sustainable Knowledge and Resources Management for Environmental Information and Computation

Claus-Peter Rückemann

Introduction

Motivation and Background

The main base for analysis and evaluation in natural sciences and environmental information is reliable, reproducible, and comparable data. The premise of any scientific procedure is that processes must be measured in order to be discussed, evaluated, and improved. Time ranges of natural and environmental processes, which mankind is aware of, span from ultrashort intervals to billions of years. With environmental processes naturally many different processes are overlaid, with different cycles.

For many problems in practical environmental research this results in time intervals of at least many decades or centuries in order to come up with suggestions or reasonable and reliable predictions. In most cases the time interval of the predictions can only span a fraction of the time the long-term data gathering itself affords. Anyhow, up to now there is no general concept with pure isolated applications available to achieve the goal of real long-term persistent knowledge.

All in all, the data and knowledge used as well as resulting from the processes and documentation should be persistently available. This means, gathering and preservation of long-term reusable data and information are among the most important tasks in the scientific workflow.

This chapter shows a new way on how structure, classification, and standardized methods can be used and integrated in order to enable long-term sustainable knowledge resources. It presents results from case studies with knowledge resources, computation, and integration. The goal and focus of this research are most complex: Long-term multidisciplinary knowledge integration and application. Therefore, the implicated theoretical frameworks and methodological backgrounds require the consideration of the greatest levels of flexibility. The chapter presents the benefits and challenges of the implemented frameworks and system components. On behalf of these facts all the required components used for the implementations described in this article have been very carefully chosen and described as flexible as necessary and as specific as possible.

Objectives: Knowledge Resources, Computation, and Integration

For the last decades, long-term knowledge resources and concepts have been created in long-term initiatives for supporting discovery and reuse of knowledge and research information. The processes include structuring, classification, and computational access. In an ongoing process knowledge objects, for example, research results, are included in the resources. The content and context creation processes are extended over an unlimited period of time. The available architecture enables to methodologically integrate and kind of material as autonomous data, references, or knowledge objects. Structure, universal classification, and references are basic features that can be exploited. The more, workflows based on the knowledge can be created for any purpose from statistics to complex knowledge discovery. As gathering of information especially in research and education is not time limited, this has not been created as a project itself. Nevertheless case studies and developments can be considered time-limited projects.

Compared to the complexity of the real world processes, the state-of-the-art in computation, namely processing, simulation, and modeling of cases and processes is very much restricted to special and simplified scenarios. Nevertheless, the computational demands are huge. This results in computing resources and architectures, which have to be suited for the needs of these purposes. The High End Computing (HEC) is an industry.

Computing resources are a valuable tool and besides in every case the architectures and requirements must be planned over years, their usage must be financed before starting this phase. In addition, any of these resources known must be used and operated economically. As there is currently no real alternative to the market-driven HEC this inherently results in several substantial drawbacks when discussing long-term initiatives. Therefore, the major objectives resulting from this background are the sustainable creation of knowledge resources and resources management especially considering multidisciplinary environmental information, computation, and integration.

This chapter is further outlined as follows: Section II introduces the topic and its background with an introduction to the state-of-the-art resources management for environmental information and computation and points to the basic principles, methodologies, and available components and standards. Section III introduces the theoretical framework and the research objectives and argumentation. Section IV discusses the research methodology including the systematics and methodology required. The core components and a prominent application are presented regarding information, computation, and integration at the case of multidisciplinary result matrices. In this section the results for long-term structure, classification, and processing for any discipline are discussed including contributions from academic research and industry. Section V provides the findings and discussion of results and evaluation, especially considering the resulting practical multidisciplinary classification for environment and climatology and the managerial and practical implications. Section VI summarizes the main results and achievements in a comprehensive conclusion.

Resources Management for Environmental Information and Computation

Some of the most challenging issues with knowledge resources are long-term vitality, universal multidisciplinary documentation, and component integration. These also include scientific data, results, and context on environment, climatology, and any associated context from research and society. Computing as well as storage are only tools and components.

Therefore, disciplines using methods, systematics, standards, and tools in a way coping best with the challenges can most probably contribute to achievements relevant for climate change, cognostics, and solutions.

Further data being publicly available can be incorporated in any way under the premise that the data formats are accessible and interfaces have been provided. An example is the CLImatological database for the World's Oceans (CLIWOC 2017). Further computational examples are wildfire control (Yin, Shaw, Wang, Carr, Berry, Gross, and Comiskey 2011), more or less isolated archaeological records (The Digital Archaeological Record 2017) and traditional collections of historical (World Digital Library 2017) and cultural information (European Cultural Heritage Online 2017). Despite any challenges, the long-term information should be accessible with scientific supercomputing resources in order to create advanced information systems and implement and improve workflows and recommended operation (Wissenschaftsrat 2011) and integration of knowledge (di Maio 2012).

The knowledge resources being part of the LX Foundation Scientific Resources (LX-Project 2017) document the references and the participated organizational bodies and projects in knowledge and resources management for environmental information and computation. These resources can integrate environmental and climatological information with any other knowledge as, for example, environmental sciences (ESSA 1968), geoscientific terms (Bates and Jackson 1980), and environmental terms and methods (Matschullat and Müller 1994; O'Riordan 1996).

Media citations can combine geoscientific and historical information and refer to 3D video animations and dioramic reconstructions as well as even to postcards, for example, linking the Volcanic Explosivity Index (VEI) (Newhall and Self 1982) resolving references to various realia (My 2007; Guardasole 2013; Bonaventura 2007).

The integration of environmental knowledge refers to many facets like turbulent diffusion in the environment (Csanady 1973), environmental chemistry and anthropogenic compounds (Hutzinger 1982), environmental information and documentation systems (Umweltbundesamt 1992), carbon dioxide (Wesoky 1997), but also on secondary context like satellites and their environments (Johnson 1965).

Knowledge resources can integrate natural sciences information with international initiatives and societal and industrial activities, which can be used for a multitude of purposes. Looking for the context of sustainable knowledge and governance aspects on environmental and climatological issues the views are naturally multidisciplinary and multinational as the following context documented within the resources shows.

The United Nations Environment Program-Global Resource Information Database (UNEP-GRID) (UNEP-GRID 2017) is collecting information on global resources.

Partnerships in Environmental Management for the Seas of East Asia (PEMSEA) (PEMSEA 2017), formerly the Sustainable Development Strategy of the Seas of East Asia (SDS-SEA), is especially focusing on governance of human activities, including their Integrated Coastal Management (ICM) activities.

The Australian Ecological Knowledge and Observation System (AEKOS) (AEKOS 2017) has done excellent basic work with the framework for Submission, Harmonization and Retrieval of Ecological Data (SHaRED) (SHaRED 2017) and the Terrestrial Ecosystem Research Network (TERN 2017).

National and international bodies are promoting environmental research and management, for example, the European Environment Agency (EEA 2017) of the European Union, the Space Environment Information System (SPENVIS) of the European Space Agency (ESA) (SPENVIS 2017), the Environmental Information System (ENVIS) (ENVIS 2017) in India, and the U.S. Environmental Protection Agency (EPA 2017). Many of them are considering universal components and widely used standards as with the Global Earth Observation System of Systems (GEOSS) (GEOSS 2017), the Infrastructure for Spatial Information in the European Community (INSPIRE), and Copernicus, The European Earth Observation Program (Copernicus 2017), formerly the Global Monitoring for the Environment and Security (GMES) (GMES 2017). With components for environmental management systems most implementations refer to the ISO 14000 on Environmental management of the International Organization for Standardization (ISO 2017).

Environmental Management and ISO Standards

The International Organization for Standardization (ISO) has published a sequence of standards on environmental management. Besides environmental management, the ISO 14000 series standards (ISO 2017) contain standard recommendation for assessment, evaluation, life cycle analysis, communication, and auditing. ISO 14000 refers to a family of voluntarily used standards and guidance documents with the ISO 14001 being the most widely used environmental management system standard worldwide.

- ISO 14001 environmental management systems–requirements with guidance for use.
- ISO 14004 environmental management systems–general guidelines on principles, systems, and support techniques.
- ISO 14006 environmental management systems–guidelines for incorporating ecodesign.
- ISO 14015 environmental assessment of sites and organizations.
- ISO 14020 series (14020 to 14025) environmental labels and declarations.
- ISO 14030 discusses postproduction environmental assessment.
- ISO 14031 environmental performance evaluation–guidelines.
- ISO 14040 series (14040 to 14049), Life Cycle Assessment (LCA). 14040 discusses preproduction planning and environment goal setting.
- ISO 14050 terms and definitions.
- ISO 14062 discusses making improvements to environmental impact goals.
- ISO 14063 environmental communication–guidelines and examples.
- ISO 14064 measuring, quantifying, and reducing greenhouse gas emissions.
- ISO 19011 specification of one audit protocol for both 14000 and 9000 series standards together.

These standards are recommended to be used internationally for Environmental Management and System (EMS) components, for comprehensive, systematic, planned, and documented implementation, including the organizational structures and resources for the implementation. Anyhow, for creating sustainable environmental knowledge resources and applications there are basic requirements for structure and consequent and consistent universal classification, which the ISO series is not supporting at the present stage. All the ISO standards are periodically reviewed by the ISO to ensure that they meet the requirements.

Present EMS is missing facilities for using a universal classification as well as an extended knowledge resources support. A major reason is that the ISO 14000 series standards are still missing to incorporate a universal long-term and multidisciplinary classification.

Besides focusing on the market requirements, trade and production processes, and information on performance improvements for internal and external stakeholders, the EMS components and ISO standards should be essentially reviewed for fostering the creation of sustainable knowledge resources and components by enabling the use of an international universal classification in this context.

Basic Principles and Methodology with ISO 14001

- *Plan* (establish objectives and processes required): Knowledge resources including a universal classification can support identifying and characterizing the initial processes, components, and products. Support is fully multidisciplinary and internationalized, spanning natural sciences, legal, and social disciplines.
- *Do* (implement the processes): The integration of structure and classification enables to describe and document the required resources, implementation, and goals. It is possible to build any workflow from this.
- *Check* (measure and monitor the processes and report results): Within this stage a periodical monitoring of the factors and performance is required. Participants' environmental targets and organizational objectives can be monitored and audited. This can help to improve processes and procedures,

for example, as done with EMS and Standards Australia or Standards New Zealand 2004.

- *Act* (take action to improve performance of EMS based on results): Following the "check stage" a scientific and operational management review is strongly suggested. This "act stage" ensures that the objectives of the EMS are being met and that they conform with best practices and legal requirements in order to cope with new developments and results.
- *Continual Improvement Process* (CIP): The concluding process, the CIP, is most important regarding the long-term perspectives. CIP in environmental management, especially with ISO 14001, differs from common quality management systems, which are quite simple. The main aspects are as follows. First, implementing EMS components in order to cover a broader range of disciplines and areas. The second aspect is to increase the support for workflows, processes, supporting products, and many associated topics. The third aspect is regularly improving collaborational and organizational frameworks, which include structures and knowledge resources.

Research Objectives and Argumentation

Environment and climate on earth has continuously changed from the beginning of the planet on. This has always been associated with most complex processes. Climate change can neither be described from a mono-disciplinary point of view nor investigated in an isolated way. Sentimental aspects as well as statements of interest groups are very common. Singular natural events and man-made factors are only a small part of the participated facets.

For the foreseeable future, simulation of scenarios and climate modeling will only be a very limited attempt to face real environment and natural sciences and societies' coherent context. The more multidisciplinary creation of knowledge has to rely on long-term sustainable resources, the more knowledge resources are in the focus. The conceptional framework is therefore dominated by conceptual knowledge and documentation, in these examples concentrating on Universal Decimal Classification (UDC).

A suitable collaboration framework has to consider the long-term multidisciplinary work on the knowledge, all aspects of use and extension of resources, and the operation of required resources. Therefore, the basic components of the multidisciplinary work are concentrating on knowledge resources, computing and storage resource, and information systems.

The knowledge resources are the most important component as they carry the long-term knowledge and investments. They represent the sustainable and long-term goals. The issues with computing and storage are becoming increasingly important with the high-end facilities for handling big data, enabling complex discovery workflows, and integrating processing, simulation, and modeling. With the high-end resources at hand and a sustainable operation it becomes feasible to create complex Integrated Information and Computing Systems (IICS).

For the objectives on improving the insights on environmental processes, climatology, geophysics, physics, geology, economy, and other associated disciplines, we need a wealth of features from the major means of documentation, information gathering, and computation.

Based on sustainable knowledge resources knowledge can be preserved and developed over decades, centuries, and presumably longer. It can integrate references to realia objects from any geological, prehistorical, and historical epoch as well as their documentation on objects, scientific and social background, and their history.

Structure, Classification, and Processing for Any Discipline

For an efficient and effective processing the knowledge data require a flexible structure and a universal systematic classification. Any knowledge resources documenting complex multidisciplinary reality for discovery applications require features for exact documentation on the one hand and they require soft criteria on the other hand.

The UDC is a classification complying with the classification criteria. Together with the content, which may deliver more detail or differing perspectives, UDC provides a universal view on the classified objects. When requiring faceted classification for multidisciplinary knowledge the universal UDC cannot be ignored as it is the most comprehensive and flexible means available and supported. With the knowledge resources in this research handling 70,000 classes, for 100,000 objects and several million referenced data the algorithms are mostly nonlinear. They allow interactive use, dynamical communication, computing, decision support, and pre- and postprocessing, for example, visualization. The basic information and classification is available in various summaries, translations, and exports (Universal Decimal Classification Consortium [UDCC] 2017; Universal Decimal Classification Summary [UDCS] 2017; Universal Decimal Classification Summary [UDCS] Translations 2017; Universal Decimal Classification Summary [UDCS] Translations: German 2017; Universal Decimal Classification Summary [UDCS] Exports 2017; Universal Decimal Classification Summary [UDCS] Linked Data 2017).

Based on this, the classification deployed for documentation (Rückemann 2012) is able to document any object with any relation, structure, and level of detail as well as intelligently selected nearby hits and references. Objects include any media, textual documents, illustrations, photos, maps, videos, sound recordings, as well as realia, physical objects such as museum objects. UDC is a suitable background classification, for example, the objects use preliminary classifications for multidisciplinary content. Standardized operations used with UDC are coordination and addition ("+"), consecutive extension ("/"), relation (":"), order-fixing ("::"), subgrouping ("[]"), non-UDC notation ("*"), alphabetic extension ("A–Z"), besides place, time, nationality, language, form, and characteristics. The small examples and unsorted excerpts of the knowledge resources objects features only refer to main UDC-based classes, which for this part of the publication are taken from the Multilingual Universal Decimal Classification Summary (UDCC Publication No. 088; Multilingual Universal Decimal Classification Summary 2012) released by the UDC Consortium under the Creative Commons Attribution Share Alike 3.0 license (Creative Commons Attribution Share Alike 2017) (first release 2009, subsequent update 2012).

Research Approaches

Research, Systematics, and Methodology

The objective is to create long-term, multidisciplinary, and multilingual knowledge resources, which provide structure and universal classification for a sustainable knowledge and resources management. The resources can classify and integrate environmental information for further use for various application scenarios, including dynamical information system components and computational components.

It must be possible to integrate and document data and information from any source. The core classification has to support multidisciplinary knowledge. The resources must be able to support various international standards, scientific methodologies, and methods. The goal is to resume data on past and present status and to mediate the essences between the so-called "precise sciences" and "humanities" for which overall success is necessary to concentrate on provable and understandable results as well as on accepted facts and testimonies of the past. The overall system has to support the definition of processes and workflows. The information is from serious research peer reviews and even more important an independent scientific auditing in addition. It is widely accepted that this is done by independent experienced scientists and not from management or disciplinary superior positions.

The methods used for classification are based on the UDC, which have their origin more than 100 years ago and the structure and environmental data samples are based on the LX Foundation Scientific Resources knowledge resources (LX-Project 2017), which are currently created and developed for more than 25 years and proofed long-term reliable and consistent.

Information, Computation, and Integration: Multidisciplinary Result Matrices

Environmental data and referred knowledge can be described with many associations and attributes. For example, with the knowledge resources a characteristic integrating request is: "environmental impact, natural variations, man-made variations, climate change." In some context it is less difficult to find near-present information, but more difficult to get the long-term multidisciplinary view. A deep discovery into the resources context is required in these cases. Primary results refer to "geology, volcano, allitic weathering, alps, climate" and secondary result point to "moon, earth axis" and to the information that the rotation of the moon and stabilization of the earth's axis also stabilized the climate for geological times. In order to get the facets of information the processing employing the UDC allows a universal faceted documentation and a large flexibility with the workflows (Rückemann 2014a).

Enabling a long-term development for the available systems components, the framework integrates Resources Oriented Architectures (ROA), Services Oriented Architectures (SOA), and "Knowledge Oriented Architectures" (KOA) (ROA 2015). In that context, many interactive and dynamical applications components, for example, mapping applications, can be used as well as batch and command line based components (Generic Mapping Tools 2017). Regarding the sustainability the framework of Knowledge Oriented Architectures (KOA) (Rückemann 2013a) is the essential component complementing SOA and ROA concepts.

The base for the implemented IICS is the collaboration house framework (Rückemann 2012b). Application components can also be integrated with the IICS regarding interactive use, advanced workflows, and code reuse (Rückemann 2011b; Rückemann 2012a; Rückemann 2013c) or complex envelopes (Rückemann 2011a; Rückemann and Gersbeck-Schierholz 2011). The integration can respect cognostic aspects of the data, for example, geocognostic views (Edwards 1996).

Workflows can be supported by intelligent system components, for example, Multi-Agent Systems (MAS) (Leitão, Inden, and Rückemann 2013; Rückemann 2013b) and handling operations systems requirements (Inden, Meridou, Papadopoulou, Anadiotis, and Rückemann 2013).

The classified knowledge objects have been used for the documentation of natural sciences research and results, for environmental and climatological information. In this context they have been investigated regarding the reconstruction of historical data, shipping routes, trade dependencies, and cultural developments. This also includes the reconstruction from archaeological data and volcanological data as well as for example the integration of meteorite data (Rückemann 2013d; Rückemann 2014a). With several case studies information referring to external archives have been successfully used in order to improve the result matrices on request, for example, with historical data by including the archives on information about Gottfried Wilhelm Leibniz (1646–1716) (LeibnizCentral 2017; GEXI 2017).

Any knowledge object classified appropriately, implicitly refers to climatological data, agricultural use, periods of climate change and multifold secondary data. The following text excerpt (Figure 3.1) from an intermediate result matrix created from object documentation shows samples of the keyword context from the index within references of the LX.

```
cite: YES 19870000 {LXK:Geology; Geosciences; Glossary}
{UDC:...} {PAGE:----..----} LXCITE://Bates:1987:Glossary
keyword-Context: IDX-ORIG :: climate
keyword-Context: IDX-ORIG :: climate classification
keyword-Context: IDX-ORIG :: climate-stratigraphic unit
keyword-Context: IDX-ORIG :: climatic
keyword-Context: IDX-ORIG :: climatic accident
keyword-Context: IDX-ORIG :: climate amelioration
keyword-Context: IDX-ORIG :: climatic deterioration
keyword-Context: IDX-ORIG :: climatic optimum
keyword-Context: IDX-ORIG :: climatic peat
keyword-Context: IDX-ORIG :: climatic province
keyword-Context: IDX-ORIG :: climatic snowtime
keyword-Context: IDX-ORIG :: climatic terrace
keyword-Context: IDX-ORIG :: climatic zone
keyword-Context: IDX-ORIG :: environment [biol]
keyword-Context: IDX-ORIG :: environment [sed]
keyword-Context: IDX-ORIG :: environmental assessment
keyword-Context: IDX-ORIG :: environmental facies
keyword-Context: IDX-ORIG :: environmental geochemistry
keyword-Context: IDX-ORIG :: environmental geology
keyword-Context: IDX-ORIG :: environmental hyperspace
                              lattice
keyword-Context: IDX-ORIG :: environmental impact
                              statement
keyword-Context: IDX-ORIG :: environmental resistance
keyword-Context: IDX-ORIG :: environmental science
cite: YES 19960000 {LXK:Umweltwissenschaften;
Umweltmanagement; Environment; Environmental Management;
```

```
Environmental Sciences} {UDC:...} {PAGE:----..----}
LXCITE://Riordan:1996:Umweltmanagement

keyword-Context: IDX-ORIG :: Umwelt

keyword-Context: IDX-ORIG :: Umweltabgaben

keyword-Context: IDX-ORIG :: Umweltbewertung

keyword-Context: IDX-ORIG :: Umweltbewußtsein

keyword-Context: IDX-ORIG :: Umweltdienstleistungen

keyword-Context: IDX-ORIG :: Umweltdiplomatie

keyword-Context: IDX-ORIG :: Umweltgesetzgebung

keyword-Context: IDX-ORIG :: Umweltgesetzgebung—Superfund-
                             Gesetzgebung

keyword-Context: IDX-ORIG :: Umweltgut

keyword-Context: IDX-ORIG :: Umweltmanagement

keyword-Context: IDX-ORIG :: Umweltökonomie

keyword-Context: IDX-ORIG :: Umweltoption

keyword-Context: IDX-ORIG :: Umweltqualitätsstandard—UQS

keyword-Context: IDX-ORIG :: Umweltrecht

keyword-Context: IDX-ORIG :: Umweltsanierung

keyword-Context: IDX-ORIG :: Umweltschäden

keyword-Context: IDX-ORIG :: Umweltschutz

keyword-Context: IDX-ORIG :: Umweltschutzbewegung

keyword-Context: IDX-ORIG :: Umweltschutzmaßnahmen

keyword-Context: IDX-ORIG :: Umweltschutzpolitik

keyword-Context: IDX-ORIG :: Umweltsteuern

keyword-Context: IDX-ORIG :: Umweltstrategie

keyword-Context: IDX-ORIG :: Umweltstreß

keyword-Context: IDX-ORIG :: Umwelttechnik

keyword-Context: IDX-ORIG :: Umweltveränderung

keyword-Context: IDX-ORIG :: Umweltverschmutzung

keyword-Context: IDX-ORIG :: Umweltverträglichkeit
                             sprüfung—UVP

keyword-Context: IDX-ORIG :: Umweltwissenschaften

cite: YES 19940000 {LXK:Geowissenschaften; Umwelt;
Geosciences; Environment} {UDC:...} {PAGE:----..----}
LXCITE://Matschullat:1994:Umwelt

keyword-Context: IDX-ORIG :: Klima
```

```
keyword-Context: IDX-ORIG :: Klimafolgenforschung

keyword-Context: IDX-ORIG :: Klimaoptimum

keyword-Context: IDX-ORIG :: Klimazustände

keyword-Context: IDX-ORIG :: Umweltfaktoren

keyword-Context: IDX-ORIG :: Umweltgefährdung

keyword-Context: IDX-ORIG :: Umweltgeologie

keyword-Context: IDX-ORIG :: Umweltgipfel

keyword-Context: IDX-ORIG :: Umweltkatastrophe

keyword-Context: IDX-ORIG :: Umweltmanagement

keyword-Context: IDX-ORIG :: Umweltmarkt

keyword-Context: IDX-ORIG :: Umweltrelevanz

keyword-Context: IDX-ORIG :: Umweltschutz

keyword-Context: IDX-ORIG :: Umweltschutzgesetze

keyword-Context: IDX-ORIG :: Umwelttechnik
```

Figure 3.1 Keyword context example from within the LX foundation scientific resources, entries from an intermediate multilingual result matrix on environment and climatology

Foundation Scientific Resources

Within the knowledge resources these index entry references resolve to the respective sources (Bates and Jackson 1980; Matschullat and Müller 1994; O'Riordan 1996). The index references cannot be handled by string search only. Advanced methods as translations services, phonetic support, and correction support can be used with the classification in order to improve the result matrix with multilanguage information on these topics. For this example an excerpt of a minimal translation support table is given in Figure 3.2.

```
climate :: Klima
climatic :: klimatisch
climatology :: Klimatologie
environment :: Umwelt
```

Figure 3.2 Practical examples of a minimal translation support table

In this case, resolving context at the index entry level means resolving expanded content, which can be considered with the discovery workflow. The result of a request supported by a translation module and filter, considering organization samples and references on environment and climatology is shown in the following excerpt of an intermediate result matrix:

2007/2/EC	[GIS, GDI, Geoinformatics, Environment, Climate, ...]:
	Directive 2007/2/EC of the European Parliament and of the Council of March 14, 2007 establishing an Infrastructure for Spatial Information in the
	European Community (INSPIRE).
2004/35/EC	[Environment, Climate, GIS, ...]:
	2004/35/EC, European Community, Environmental Liability Directive.
A2C2	[Environment, Climate]:
	Albay in Action on Climate Change.
AAOE	[Meteorology, Climate]:
	Airborne Antarctic Ozone Experiment.
ACC	[Environment, Climate, Oceanography]:
	Anthropogenic Climate Change.
ACCAD	[Climatology, Oceanography, Committee]:
	Advisory Committee on Climate Applications and Data (CCl).
ACSYS	[Oceanography, Climatology]:
	Arctic Climate System Study (WCRP).
ADIOS	[Climate, Oceanography]:
	Asian Dust Input to the Oceanic System.
AEIDC	[Climatology, Environment, Oceanography]:
	Arctic Environmental Information and Data Centre, United States.
AEKOS	[Environment, Climate, GIS, ...]:
	The Australian Ecological Knowledge and Observation System, Australia.
AGCM	[Oceanography]:
	Atmospheric General Circulation Model.
AMOC	[Oceanography, Climatology]:
	Atlantic Meridional Overturning Circulation.

APARE   [Oceanography]:

             East Asian-North Pacific Regional Experiment.

ASEAMS   [Oceanography, Association]:

             Association of South-East Asian Marine Scientists.

BUIS   [Environment, Climate, GIS, ...]:

             Betriebliche Umweltinformationssysteme.

CCl   [Climate, Oceanography, Commission]:

             Commission for Climatology (WMO).

CCOP   [Oceanography, Committee, Mining]:

             Committee for Coordination of Joint Prospecting for Mineral Resources in

             Asian Offshore Areas.

CIP   [Environment, Climate, GIS, ...]:

             Continual Improvement Process.

Copernicus   [Environment, Climate, GIS, ...]:

             European EO Program.

             European Earth Observation Program.

EAHC   [Oceanography, Hydrography, Commission]:

             East Asia Hydrographic Commission (IHO).

EEA   [Environment, Climate, GIS, ...]:

             European Environment Agency, European Union.

EIONET   [Environment, Climate, GIS, ...]:

             European Environment Information and Observation NETwork.

EIS   [Environment, Climate, GIS, ...]:

             Environmental Information System

ELD   [Environment, Climate, GIS, ...]:

             Environmental Liability Directive. 2004/35/EC, European Community.

EMS   [Environment, Climate, GIS, ...]:

             Environmental Management System.

ENVIS   [Environment, Climate, GIS, ...]:

             Environmental Information System, India.

EPA   [Environment, Climate, GIS, ...]:

             U.S. Environmental Protection Agency.

EUA   [Environment, Climate, GIS, ...]:

             Europäische Umweltagentur.

FAOB	[Abbreviation]:
	Federation of Asian and Oceanian Biochemists.
FIRE	[Climatology]:
	First ISLSCP Regional Experiment.
GEOSS	[Environment, Climate, GIS, ...]:
	Global Earth Observation System of Systems.
GMCC	[Institute, Geophysics, Environment, Climate]:
	Geophysical Monitoring for Climatic Change.
GMES	[Environment, Climate, GIS, ...]:
	Global Monitoring for Environment and Security.
GOOS	[Environment, Climate, GIS, ...]:
	Global Ocean Observing System.
GPCC	[Climate]:
	Global Precipitation Climatology Center.
GPCP	[Oceanography]:
	Global Precipitation Climatology Project (WCRP).
IMIS	[Environment, Climate, GIS, ...]:
	Integriertes Mess- und Informationssystem.
INSPIRE	[Environment, Climate, GIS, ...]:
	Infrastructure for Spatial Information in the European Community. 2007/2/EC,
	European Community.
ISCCP	[Satellite, Climate]:
	International Satellite Cloud Climatology Project (WCRP).
ISLSCP	[Climatology, Oceanography]:
	International Satellite Land Surface Climatology Project (WCRP).
ISO 14000	[Environment, Standards]: ...
ISO 14000	[Environmental Management]: ...
LCA	[Environment, Climate, GIS, ...]:
	Life Cycle Assessment.
SEARNG	[Environment, Geophysics]:
	S.E. Asian Region Network for Geosciences.
SHaRED	[Environment, Climate, GIS, ...]:
	Submission, Harmonization and Retrieval of Ecological Data (tool).

SHIFOR   [Oceanography]:

              A climatology and persistence model.

              (not an acronym).

SPENVIS   [Environment, Climate, GIS, ...]:

              The Space Environment Information System, ESA.

SRBCP   [Climatology, Satellite, Oceanography]:

              Satellite Radiation Budget Climatology Project (WCRP).

TEK   [Environment, Climate, GIS, ...]:

              Traditional Ecological Knowledge.

TERN   [Environment, Climate, GIS, ...]:

              Terrestrial Ecosystem Research Network, Australia.

UEUS   [Environment, Climate, GIS, ...]:

              Umweltbezogene Entscheidungsunterstützungssysteme.

UIS   [Environment, Climate, GIS, ...]:

              Umweltinformationssystem.

UNEP   [Environment, Climate, GIS, ...]:

              United Nations Environment Program.

UNEP-GRID   [Environment, Climate, GIS, ...]:

              United Nations Environment Program/Global Resource
              Information Database.

USM   [Environment, Climate, GIS, ...]:

              Umweltbezogene Instrumente des Strategischen
              Managements.

WCED   [Environment, Climate, GIS, ...]:

              World Commission on Environment and Development.

WCRP   [Climatology, Oceanography, ...]:

              World Climate Research Program.

This small excerpt shows only some main entries from a result matrix. The entries shown list some main information on the acronyms, abbreviations, and alike as well as the broad spectrum and actual and historical range of the references. A full result matrix can contain projects, centers, institutions, terms, and all their references, links, and secondary information.

The references and especially the classification have been left out here in order to concentrate on the disciplinary topics within the results. For example, especially the Directive 2007/2/EC of the European Parliament and of the Council of March 14, 2007 establishing an Infrastructure for Spatial Information in the European Community (INSPIRE) is closely coupled with environmental protection, environmental legislation, and environmental monitoring (INSPIRE 2017).

The knowledge resources associate 2007/2/EC with the Directive 2004/35/EC, the Environmental Liability Directive (ELD), due to the environmental relevance (EC 2004; EC 2007).

The matrix can contain not only the disciplinary relevant references on content and context but also the associated topics from interactive online discovery via learning processes, for example, on traditional ecological knowledge (Casimirri 2003).

A secondary view can, for example, document the change on the meaning of certain terms over time and refer to the appropriate context. The U.S. Environmental Science Services Administration (ESSA) defined environmental science in 1968 "A science that is involved with 'all of nature we perceive or can observe, that is our physical environment-a composite of earth, sun, sea, and atmosphere, their interactions, and the hazards they present'" (Bates and Jackson 1980). Bates and Jackson summarize "Earth science applied to the human habitat." Later nondiscipline-centered definitions more and more refer to human environment and man-made interactions and changes.

A practical example of top associated terms from above objects in the intermediate result matrix created from the knowledge resources applying the classification is shown in Figure 3.3.

The references deliver the links, for example, to the objects volcano, Vesuvius, Campi Flegrei, phlegra, scene of fire, Pompeji, Herculaneum, volcanic ash, lapilli, catastrophe, climatology, eruption, lava, gas ejection, CO_2, and so on. In turn these links, for example, contribute with detailed disciplinary content and context references (Figure 3.4) to the result matrix on the environmental request.

The excerpt of this entry (Figure 3.4) from the knowledge resources refers to classifications, for example, UDC, keywords, synonyms,

```
Antarctica

Climatology

Climate Change

Environmental Sciences

Glaciology

Oceanography

Volcanology

...
```

Figure 3.3 Practical examples of top associated terms in the intermediate result matrix

```
Vesuvius [Volcanology, Geology, Archaeology]:

        (lat.) Mons Vesuvius.

        (ital.) Vesuvio.

        (deutsch.) Vesuv.

        Volcano, Gulf of Naples, Italy.

        Complex volcano (compound volcano).

        Stratovolcano, large cone (Gran Cono).

        Volcano Type: Somma volcano,

        VNUM: 0101-02=,

        Summit Elevation: 1281\UD{m}.

        The volcanic activity in the region is observed by
        the Oservatorio

        Vesuviano. The Vesuvius area has been declared a
        national park on

        \isodate{1995}{06}{05}. The most known antique
        settlements at the Vesuvius are Pompeji and
        Herculaneum.

        Syn.: Vesaevus, Vesevus, Vesbius, Vesvius

        s. volcano, super volcano, compound volcano

        s. also Pompeji, Herculaneum, seismology

        ...

        compare La Soufrière, Mt. Scenery, Soufriere

        %%IML: UDC:[911.2+55]:[57+930.85]:[902]"63"
```

```
(4+23+24)=12=14

%%IML: GoogleMapsLocation: http://maps.google.de/
maps?...ll=40.821961,14.428868...
```

Figure 3.4 Excerpt of knowledge resources object entry including classifications, keywords, geo-locations, and references

geo-locations, and references, which allow the application of advanced processing, mapping, statistics, heuristic methods, phonetic algorithms, translations, and many more. Classification, content, and context can be evaluated together and refer to contributions from integrated and distributed information resources.

Contributions to Computational Resources from Academic Research and Industry

The activities in research are multifold but they strongly depend on funding. Political and social activities are reacting on demands from society and economy. The resources providers and computing industry are providing capacities, creating architectures, and selling their products. New resources and architectures are produced and products and services are mostly produced and sold for those best paying. The triangle of that constellation can be summarized with some examples:

- *Scientific disciplines:* Basic research, systematics, methodologies, multidisciplinary research, ...
- *Political activities:* Strategies, funding, legal regulations, ...
- *Resources providers, computing industry, engineering:* Developing new architectures, providing technological strategies, creating resources, low level interfaces ...

Concentrating on the contributions for advanced processing and computing using knowledge resources in the fields of environmental sciences shows a hiatus in sustainability between long-term methodological means and technological strategies.

Technological strategies are underlying regular short-term replacement cycles (e.g., hardware, architectures, programming environments).

With these, resources providers and industry frequently change their portfolio of affordable supplies depending mostly only on the top quantity of consumer demands.

Methodological approaches like documentation, simulation, and modeling are in the hands of research disciplines, which struggle with sufficient continuity in their processes in order to cope with the costs and challenges even for short time intervals like 6 to 15 years. The institutions far most widely involved in big data handling and long-term knowledge worldwide are libraries and museums on the on hand and search engines on the other hand.

Besides many more restrictions, libraries are concentrating on a limited spectrum of objects, mostly "written" objects. Museums are strongly limited by the quantity they can handle. Search engines mostly operate on unstructured data, which they do not maintain or develop themselves, neither for structure, content nor for long-term aspects. Overall, the knowledge available for possible long-term activities is extremely heterogeneous and fragmentary resulting from the limitation in variety, structure, consistency, and continuance.

The requirements for making use of such data for large implementations are even less demanding and up to now resulted in simple search and request facilities based on the already available data, which even cannot take real advantage neither of the knowledge nor the computational potential.

In contrast to that, the preliminary academically work and achievements would allow to conceptualize a much more universal and sustainable approach to long-term knowledge. Methodological means have been successfully developed, implemented in various components, and used for decades, for example, for phonetics, statistics, pseudonyms, ligature handling, translations, transcriptions, transliterations, and typographical corrections.

A large number of long-term, multidisciplinary case studies in natural sciences and humanities have shown the efficient integration of systematically and methodological approaches with knowledge resources and universal classification and scientific and FEC (Rückemann 2013d, 2014b).

The available algorithms, frameworks, and tools are numberless. Anyhow, the number of sustainable components, which can in fact be used for long-term resources is quite restricted (Russel and O'Dell 1918; Knuth 1973; National Archives and Records Administration—NARA 2007; Stok 1994; LX-Project SNDX 2017; Rempel 1998; Kupries 2003; ECHO 2017; GMT 2017; GDAL Development Team 2017; Open-MPI 2017; Tcl Developer Site 2017; CTAN 2017).

In all major cases for creating and operating complex long-term resources the efforts for creating the content have shown to be extremely high but also the most rewarding long-term contribution. One of the most frequently used application scenarios, which can be discussed based on some general understanding, is the computation of result matrices within complex knowledge discovery or simple search requests. This includes compute requests, resources' integration, and workflow creation based on contributions from disciplines, services, and resources' providers. The goal within this scenario is the creation of result matrices from available knowledge resources utilizing available means.

Computing result matrices is an arbitrary complex task, which can depend on various factors. Applying statistics and classification to knowledge resources has successfully provided excellent solutions, which can be used for optimizing result matrices in context of natural sciences, for example, geosciences, archaeology, volcanology or with spatial disciplines, as well as for universal knowledge (Rückemann 2014c, 2015). The method and application types used for optimization imply some general characteristics when putting discovery workflows into practice regarding components like terms, media, and other context (Table 3.1).

For the study, the number of result matrix entries has been defined to 10 based on 50,000 objects. The number of common workflow operations

Table 3.1 Resulting per-instance-calls for types of methods and applications used for optimization with knowledge discovery

Type	Terms	Media	Workflow	Algorithm	Combination
Mean	500	20	20	50,000	3,000
Median	10	5	2	5,000	50
Deviation	30	5	5	200	20
Distribution	90	40	15	20	120
Correlation	15	10	5	20	90
Probability	140	15	20	50	150
Phonetics	50	5	10	20	50

Regular expressions	920	100	50	40	1,500
References	720	120	30	5	900
Association	610	60	10	5	420
UDC	530	120	20	5	660
Keywords	820	100	10	5	600
Translations	245	20	5	5	650
Corrections	60	10	5	5	150
External resources	40	30	5	5	40

is in the range of 6,500 with according wall time on one core of about 6,700 seconds. Result matrices generated with special focus, so called "Section Views," have shown to be dominated by prominent features, the most often used, for example, in combination are time, space, disciplines, attributes, and culture.

Statistics methods have shown to be an important means for successfully optimizing result matrices. The most widely implemented methods for the creation of result matrices are intermediate result matrices based on regular expressions and intermediate result matrices based on combined regular expressions, classification, and statistics, giving their numbers special weight. Based on these per-instance numbers this results in demanding requirements for complex applications–On "numerical data": Millions of calls are done per algorithm and dataset, hundreds in parallel or compact numeric routines. On "terms": Hundred thousands of calls are done per sub-workflow, thousands in parallel or complex routines, are done. Most resources are used for one application scenario only. Only 5 to 10 percent overlaps between disciplines–due to mostly isolated use. Large benefits result from multidisciplinary multilingual integration. The multilingual application adds an additional dimension to the knowledge matrix, which can be used by most discovery processes. As this implemented dimension is of very high quality the matrix space can benefit vastly from content and references. Still, sustainable long-term efforts have to focus on long-term knowledge creation, integrated systems, and complex knowledge discovery.

The importance of scalable workflows is well demonstrated when computing optimized result matrices for the processing of objects from knowledge resources (Rückemann 2014c), which increases the effectiveness and quality of results while reducing the resources' requirements. A simple workflow can be exemplary summarized with several steps:

- Knowledge base request
- Keyword filtering
- Object processing
- UDC filtering
- Object element processing
- Object container retrieval
- Media retrieval
- Media processing
- Container processing
- Building resulting media
- Visualization
- Provisioning results

Currently there is no publicly supported sustainable long-term funding for the required long-term resources. The driving forces are not coming from the industry itself, this is expected to be done by disciplines, funding agencies, governmental as well as intergovernmental or transgovernmental initiatives. In the future, a stronger and more sustainable collaboration between disciplines, services, and resources providers is required in order to interlink the systematically creation, the methodological implementation, and the sustainable support. This includes political activities on all levels, creating a reliable and sustainable collaboration environment.

Classification for Interlinking Any Multidisciplinary Knowledge

UDC is an excellent classification for interlinking any multidisciplinary knowledge including all disciplines and facets. UDC is currently used by about 150,000 institutions worldwide, many in classifying catalogue context. The integration of UDC classification with long-term knowledge resources is of major benefit for an efficient and sustainable use and long-term vitality of the knowledge as has been shown by all cited practical case studies.

It has been shown how long-term knowledge resources can be created and used for more than 25 years considering content and context with sophisticated workflows implementing various technologies over the years. The knowledge resources have proven to provide a universal way of describing multidisciplinary objects, expressing relations between any kind of objects and data, for example, from archaeology, geosciences, and natural sciences as well as defining workflows for calculation and computation for application components. Systematically structuring, classification, as well as soft "silken" criteria with LX and UDC support have provided efficient and economic means for using information system components and supercomputing resources. With these, the solution scales, for example, regarding references, resolution, and view arrangements even with big data scenarios and parallel computing resources. The components and resources have shown highest extensibility, from knowledge and content perspective as well as from application side.

The creation of long-term knowledge resources and applications derived do benefit vastly from this universal integration of multidisciplinary and long-range content and context information. Regarding the environmental disciplines multidisciplinary can mean natural sciences, humanities, industry, and economy. The long-range information is prehistorical, historical, and archaeological information and the context information are, for example, associations, references, and knowledge objects. The concept can be transferred to numerous applications in a very flexible way and has shown to be most sustainable. The successful integration of IICS components and advanced scientific computing based on structured information and faceted classification of objects has provided a very flexible and extensible solution for the implementation of climatological information systems as well as for archaeological information systems.

Resulting Multidisciplinary Classification for Environment and Climatology

The conceptual knowledge related result of this research is practical classification for environment and climatology (Table 3.2, see Annex). This table shows a classification, which can be integrated with the knowledge resources. This example shows a small excerpt of referred and practically usable UDC codes to be associated the objects. The excerpt includes a range of environmental and climatological topics. Contributions to these multidisciplinary topics are from a very wide range of fields. The context of climatology is naturally multidisciplinary, integrating many disciplines, phenomena, and secondary and tertiary aspects. The full range of classifications and billions of combined classifications and facets can be used with any knowledge resources objects, containers, and other means of creating groups. This small excerpt already shows very well how interweaved the climatological, natural sciences, and social sciences are. The main focus is on climatological aspects, environmental issues, as well as on natural sciences and social sciences topics. All the entries can be combined following the UDC rules for creating complex and faceted classifications as well as creating any number of classification views for an object or a group of objects.

Managerial and Practical Implications

Developments in multidisciplinary knowledge can be consistently handled and managed with the steadily evolving classification editions. These can be used in production with the knowledge resources for long-term documentation. The resources and documentation can be multidisciplinary to any extent, fully multilingual, and it can be kept consistent supporting classification editions.

In addition, with a multidisciplinary collaboration framework any application and operation scenario can be supported. As with sustainable long-term strategies, it has been found that with multidisciplinary research the funding of researchers should complement the funding of institutions. Supporting knowledge creation and research at the central researcher and collaboration level is a core requirement for a sustainable long-term knowledge creation and discovery.

It has been demonstrated with case studies over the last years that archaeological and environmental IICS can provide advanced multidisciplinary information as from climatology, archaeology, and geosciences by means of HEC resources. The basic architecture has been created using the collaboration house framework, long-term documentation and classification of objects, flexible algorithms, workflows, and active source components. As shown with the examples, any kind of computing request, for example, discovery, data retrieval, visualization, and processing, can be done from the application components accessing the knowledge resources. Computing interfaces can carry any interactive or batch job description. Anyhow, the hardware and system resources have to be configured appropriately for a use with the workflow. For future applications a kind of "tooth system" for long-term documentation and algorithms for use with IICS and the exploitation of supercomputing resources will be developed. Besides this, it is intended to further extend the content spectrum of the knowledge resources.

Conclusion

Long-term knowledge resources, systematics, and methodology as resulting from this research have shown to provide sustainable and efficient means of documenting, gathering, integrating, reusing, and managing any kind of information. For multidisciplinary research, for example, environmental studies including natural sciences and social sciences context, the knowledge resources support the multidisciplinary knowledge gathering and documentation as well as classification, discovery, and decision-making processes. Implicitly, this is also of huge importance for creating sustainable EMS and information system components based on long-term resources and standardized components. For a sustainable creation of multidisciplinary long-term knowledge it is suggested to have a complementary personalized funding of researchers in addition to the funding of institutions. Knowledge, for example, data or workflow objects, can be created and used for long periods of time contributing to the multidisciplinary integration essentially required for environmental research.

The research and the reasons for climate change effects are multifold. Anthropogenic factors include technological and industrial development. Many aspects and interests, for example, economic, lobby, or network interests, are often contrary to ecological aspects. Contributions can be based on provable natural sciences facts or on the other hand argumentation can be nonscientific. This results in multidisciplinary challenges for documentation as well as for analysis of information.

The use of UDC and knowledge resources with multidisciplinary context can be recommended with any climatology, environmental, and related disciplines. The case studies have shown that the knowledge resources can be efficiently created, used, and extended for sustainable long-term documentation and application components.

Advanced long-term knowledge resources integrating structure and universal classification can successfully provide any information and interlink all the required disciplines and context helping to document and integrate any multidisciplinary knowledge with environmental and climatological application scenarios. Knowledge resources can, for example, deliver references within knowledge, acronym expansions, translations, directives, publication content and context, realia references, media samples. The concept and components are multilingual, support big data on volume, variability, velocity, and vitality, and can be used with HEC–distributed and supercomputing–resources. More than that, the knowledge resources can support data and application assignments as well as application and computing and storage system assignments.

With the systematics and methodological background from scientific research, there are large numbers of basic components, algorithms, and frameworks available from advanced scientific computing and HEC, which are technically well supported by the computing industry. Nevertheless, the triangle of the constellation of scientific disciplines, political activities, and resources providers, computing industry, and engineering in future requires a strong and sustainable collaboration support between disciplines, services, and resources providers.

A lot of environmental, natural sciences, and archaeological topics have been addressed with the last years' research and developments. Objects and components of any related topics be classified and integrated. There are three major targets for sustainability and long-term vitality: Knowledge resources, consistent universal classification, and multidisciplinary content, for example, on environmental research, results, term, recommendations, best practices, and legal regulations. The primary operational facilities include big data access, internationalization, and multilingual classification. Regarding complexity the deployment of intelligent system components and methods for analysis and advanced discovery has been found very beneficial.

The major benefits of the efforts correlate with the major challenges from the required combination of the components: These challenges are integration and the long-term aspects, for example, the operation of the resources, the integration of components, and the consistency of heterogeneous contributions. On the other side the integrated architectures are designed to eliminate most conceptual limitations. Challenges can mostly arise from a different understanding of real world complexity and from creation and operation of technical implementations on that restricted base. We may suggest that sufficient sustainable holistic and long-term funding can provide a reliable base for future research and education on the ongoing creation and universal utilization of universal knowledge resources.

Acknowledgment

I am grateful to my scientific colleagues at the Westfälische Wilhelms-Universität Münster (WWU) and to the "Knowledge in Motion" (KiM) long-term projects, Unabhängiges Deutsches Institut für Multidisziplinäre Forschung (DIMF), for partially funding this implementation, case study, and publication (grant D2012F2P04492) and to its senior scientific members, especially to Dr. Friedrich Hülsmann, Gottfried Wilhelm Leibniz Bibliothek (GWLB) Hannover, to Dipl.-Biol. Birgit Gersbeck-Schierholz, Leibniz Universität Hannover, and to Dipl.-Ing. Martin Hofmeister, Hannover, for fruitful discussion, inspiration, practical multidisciplinary case studies, and the analysis of advanced concepts. I am grateful to all national and international academic, industry, and business partners in the GEXI and LX Cooperations for the innovative constructive work and the Science and High Performance Supercomputing Centre (SHPSC) for long-term support of collaborative research and the LX-Project for providing suitable resources. Heartfelt thanks to the members of the boards and the participants of the INFOCOMP, GEOProcessing, ICDS/DigitalWorld, and ICNAAM conferences for their excellent collaboration within the last years. Many thanks to the scientific colleagues at the WWU and the Institute for Legal Informatics (IRI), Leibniz Universität Hannover, sharing experiences on ZIV, HLRN, Grid, and Cloud resources and for participating in fruitful

case studies as well as the participants of the EULISP Program for pro-
lific scientific discussion over the last years. I am grateful to the UDC
Consortium for continuously providing, extending, and improving the
excellent UDC for public use. I am grateful to the Gottfried Wilhelm
Leibniz Bibliothek (GWLB), Hannover, Germany, for the collection and
public provisioning of most complete information on Gottfried Wilhelm
Leibniz and related work. Thanks go to the Akademie der Wissenschaften
zu Göttingen and the Akademie der Wissenschaften zu Berlin for the
successful implementation of information system components enabling
an advanced provisioning and integration of information. I do thank the
international colleagues from geosciences, informatics, and archaeology
in the present collaborations and the peer reviewers for constructive feedback and proof-reading this chapter.

References

AEKOS (Australian Ecological Knowledge and Observation System). 2017. *The Australian Ecological Knowledge and Observation System*. Australia, Retrieved from http://aekos.org.au/

Bates, R.L., and J. Jackson, eds. 1980. *Glossary of Geology: American Geological Institute*, 2nd ed. Virginia: Falls Church.

Bonaventura, M.A.L. 2007. *Pompeii Reconstructed Book with DVD*. Rome: Archeolibri. ISBN: 978-8-89551-223-5.

Casimirri, G. 2003. "Problems with Integrating Traditional Ecological Knowledge into Contemporary Resource Management." Original unedited version of a paper submitted to the XXI World Forestry Congress, Quebec City, Canada, Retrieved from http://fao.org/docrep/ARTICLE/WFC/XII/0887-A3.HTM

Creative Commons Attribution Share Alike. 2017. "Creative Commons Attribution Share Alike 3.0 license." http://creativecommons.org/licenses/by-sa/3.0/

CLIWOC (CLImatological Database for the World's Oceans). 2017. "Climatological Database for the World's Oceans 1750–1850." http://pendientedemigracion. ucm.es/info/cliwoc/

Copernicus, N. 2017. "Copernicus, European Earth Observation Programme." http://copernicus.eu/

Csanady, G.T. 1973. *Turbulent Diffusion in the Environment*, Vol. 3 of Geophysics and Astrophysics Monographs. Dordrecht: D. Reidel Publishing Company.

CTAN (Comprehensive TeX Archive Network). 2017. "Comprehensive TeX Archive Network." (TeX/LaTeX), Retrieved from http://ctan.org (March 8, 2017)

di Maio, P. 2012. "A Global Vision: Integrating Community Networks Knowledge." *In Community Wireless Symposium, European Community.* Barcelona: EC Infoday, October 5, 2012 Retrieved from http://people. ac.upc.edu/leandro/misc/CAPS_Paola.pdf

EC. 2004. Directive 2004/35/EC. European Community. Directive 2004/35/ EC, Environmental Liability Directive.

EC. 2007. Directive 2007/2/EC. European Community. Directive 2007/2/EC of the European Parliament and of the Council of March 14, 2007 Establishing an Infrastructure for Spatial Information in the European Community (INSPIRE).

Edwards, G. 1996. "Geocognostics—A New Paradigm for Spatial Information?" In *Proceedings of the AAAI Spring Symposium.*

EEA (European Environment Agency). 2017. *European Environment Agency.* Copenhagen, Denmark: European Union. http://europa.eu/about-eu/ agencies/regulatoryagenciesbodies/policyagencies/eea/indexdd.ht m

ENVIS (Environmental Information System). 2017. *Environmental Information System*, India. http://envis.nic.in/

EPA (Environmental Protection Agency). 2017. U.S. *Environmental Protection Agency.* Retrieved from http://epa.gov/

ESSA (Environmental Science Services Administration). 1968. *U.S. Environmental Science Services Administration.* Washington, DC: U.S. Government Printing Office.

ECHO (European Cultural Heritage Online). 2017. *Max-Planck Institut für Wissenschaftsgeschichte* (English: Max Planck Institute for the History of Science). Berlin. http://echo.mpiwg-berlin.mpg.de/

GDAL Development Team. 2017. *GDAL—Geospatial Data Abstraction Library.* Open Source Geospatial Foundation, Retrieved from http://gdal.org

GMT (Generic Mapping Tools). 2017. *Generic Mapping Tools,* Retrieved from http://imina.soest.hawaii.edu/gmt

GEOSS (Global Earth Observation System of Systems). 2017. *Global Earth Observation System of Systems,* Retrieved from http://earthobservations.org

GEXI (Geo Exploration and Information). 2017. *Geo Exploration and Information*, Retrieved from http://user.uni-hannover.de/cpr/x/rprojs/de/#gexi

GMES (Global Monitoring for the Environment and Security). 2017. *Global Monitoring for the Environment and Security*, Retrieved from http://ec.europa. eu/enterprise/policies/space/gmes/

Guardasole. 2013. Vesuvio 1270 m. Guardasole SRL, Napoli, Via Argine, 313, Italia, 2013, Postcard, 40067, Description: 1944 Eruptions and Present Day Crater. Collection: LX, Provider: BGS, Entry date: 2013.

Hutzinger, O, ed. 1982. *The Handbook of Environmental Chemistry— Anthropogenic Compounds.* 3 vols, Part B. Berlin, Heidelberg, and New York, NY: Springer Verlag.

Inden, U., D.T. Meridou, M.E.C. Papadopoulou, A.C.G. Anadiotis, and C.-P. Rückemann. 2013. "Complex Landscapes of Risk in Operations Systems Aspects of Processing and Modelling." In *Proceedings of The Third International Conference on Advanced Communications and Computation (INFOCOMP 2013)*, November 17–22, pp. 99–104. Lisbon, Portugal: XPS Press. Retrieved from http://thinkmind.org/index.php?view=article&articleid=infocomp_2013_5_10_10114

INSPIRE (Infrastructure for Spatial Information in Europe). 2017. *Infrastructure for Spatial Information in Europe*, Retrieved from http://inspire.jrc.ec.europa.eu/

ISO (International Organisation for Standardisation). 2017. *ISO 14000— Environmental Management. International Organisation for Standardisation*, Retrieved from http://iso.org/iso/iso14000

Johnson, F.S. 1965. *Satellite Environment Handbook*. California, USA: Stanford.

Knuth, D.E. 1973. *The Art of Computer Programming: Sorting and Searching*, 3 Vols. Redwood City, CA: Addison-Wesley.

Kupries, A. 2003. *tcllib, soundex.tcl, Soundex Tcl Port Documentation*. (code after Donald E. Knuth).

Leibniz Central. 2017. *Gottfried Wilhelm Leibniz Bibliothek (GWLB)*. Hannover: Niedersächsische Landesbibliothek. http://leibnizcentral.de

Leitão, P., U. Inden, and C.-P. Rückemann. 2013. "Parallelising Multi-agent Systems for High Performance Computing." In *Proceedings of The Third International Conference on Advanced Communications and Computation (INFOCOMP 2013)*, November 17–22, pp. 1–6. Lisbon, Portugal: XPS Press. http://thinkmind.org/download.php? articleid=infocomp_2013_1_10_10055

LX-Project. 2017. *LX-Project,* Retrieved from http://user.uni-hannover.de/cpr/x/rprojs/en/#LX

LX-Project SNDX. 2017. LX-SNDX, a Soundex Module Concept for Knowledge Resources. LX-Project Consortium Technical Report, Retrieved from http://user.uni-hannover.de/cpr/x/rprojs/en/#LX

Matschullat, J., and G. Müller, eds. 1994. *Geowissenschaften und Umwelt*. Berlin, Heidelberg, and Germany: Springer-Verlag.

Multilingual Universal Decimal Classification Summary. 2012. *UDC Consortium, Web resource, v. 1.1*. The Hague: UDC Consortium (UDCC Publication No. 088). Retrieved from http://udcc.org/udcsummary/php/index.php

NARA (National Archives and Records Administration). 2007. *The Soundex Indexing System*. (2007-05-30). Retrieved from http://archives.gov/research/cen sus/soundex.html

Newhall, C.G., and S. Self. 1982. "The Volcanic Explosivity Index (VEI): An Estimate of Explosive Magnitude for Historical Volcanism." *Journal Geophysical Research* 87, pp. 1231–38.

Open-MPI. 2017. *Open-MPI.* Retrieved from http://open-mpi.org (March 8, 2017)

O'Riordan, T, ed. 1996. *Umweltwissenschaften und Umweltmanagement: Ein interdisziplinäres Lehrbuch.* Berlin, Germany: Springer.

PEMSEA (Partnerships in Environmental Management for the Seas of East Asia). 2017. *Partnerships in Environmental Management for the Seas of East Asia,* Retrieved from http://pemsea.org

Bonaventura, M.A.L. 2007. *Pompeii Reconstructed Book with DVD.* Archeolibri.

Rempel, E. 1998. tcllib, soundex.tcl, Soundex Tcl Port. (code after Donald E. Knuth).

ROA (Resource-Oriented Architecture). 2015. *Resource-Oriented Architecture,* Retrieved from http://en.wikipedia.org/wiki/Resource-oriented_architecture

Rückemann, C.-P. 2011a. "Envelope Interfaces for Geoscientific Processing with High Performance Computing and Information Systems." In *Proceedings International Conference on Advanced Geographic Information Systems, Applications, and Services (GEOProcessing 2011),* February 23–28, pp. 23–28. [Rückemann, C.-P. and Wolfson, O. (eds.)] Gosier, Guadeloupe, France: DigitalWorld, XPS, Xpert Publishing Solutions. Retrieved from http://thinkmind.org/download.php?articleid=geoprocessing_2011_2_10_30030

Rückemann, C.-P. 2011b. "Application and High Performant Computation of Fresnel Sections." In *Symposium on Advanced Computation and Information in Natural and Applied Sciences, Proceedings of The 9th International Conference on Numerical Analysis and Applied Mathematics (ICNAAM),* September 19–25, Vol. 1389, no. 1, pp. 1268–71, Halkidiki, Greece, Proceedings of the American Institute of Physics (AIP), Melville, New York: AIP Press, American Institute of Physics. Retrieved from http://link.aip.org/link/?APCPCS/1389/1268/1 (Permalink)

Rückemann, C.-P. 2012a. "Supercomputing Resources Empowering Superstack with Interactive and Integrated Systems." In *The Second Symposium on Advanced Computation and Information in Natural and Applied Sciences, Proceedings of The 10th International Conference on Numerical Analysis and Applied Mathematics (ICNAAM),* September 19–25, Vol. 1479, no. 1, pp. 873–76. Kos, Greece, Proceedings of the American Institute of Physics (AIP), Melville, New York, NY: AIP Press, American Institute of Physics (American Institute of Physics Conference Proceedings). Retrieved from http://link.aip.org/link/apcpcs/v1479/i1/p873/s1 (Permalink)

Rückemann, C.-P. 2012b. "Integrating Information Systems and Scientific Computing." *International Journal on Advances in Systems and Measurements* 5, nos. 3–4, pp. 113–27. http://thinkmind.org/index.php?view=article&articleid=sysmea_v5_n34_2012_3/

Rückemann, C.-P. 2013a. "Sustainable Knowledge Resources Supporting Scientific Supercomputing for Archaeological and Geoscientific Information

Systems." In *Proceedings of The Third International Conference on Advanced Communications and Computation (INFOCOMP 2013)*, November 17–22, pp. 55–60. Lisbon, Portugal: XPS Press, ISSN: 2308-3484, ISBN-13: 978-1-61208-310-0, Retrieved from http://thinkmind.org/index.php?view= article&articleid=infocomp_2013_3_20_10034

Rückemann, C.-P. 2013b. "High End Computing and Advanced Scientific Supercomputing: Sustainability, Challenges, and Prospects with Management and Research, Lecture, International Expert Panel on Exa-Intelligence: Next Generations of Intelligent Multi-Agent and High End Computing Systems in Development and Practice." In *The Third International Conference on Advanced Communications and Computation (INFOCOMP 2013)*, November 18, 2013. Lisbon, Portugal: Retrieved November 17–22, 2013 from http://iaria. org/conferences2013/filesINFOCOMP13/INFOCOMP2013_EXPERT_ PANEL. pdf

Rückemann, C.-P. 2013c. "High End Computing for Diffraction Amplitudes." In *The Third Symposium on Advanced Computation and Information in Natural and Applied Sciences, Proceedings of The 11th International Conference of Numerical Analysis and Applied Mathematics (ICNAAM)*, September 21–27, 2013, Rhodes, Greece: Proceedings of the American Institute of Physics (AIP), Volume 1558, Part 1, pages 305–08. AIP Press, American Institute of Physics, Melville, New York, USA, Oktober 2013. ISBN-13: 978-0-7354-1184-5, ISSN: 0094-243X (American Institute of Physics Conference Proceedings, print), DOI: 10.1063/1.4825483, Retrieved from http://link. aip.org/ link/?APCPCS/1558/ 305/1 (Permalink).

Rückemann, C.-P. 2013d. "High End Computing Using Advanced Archaeology and Geoscience Objects." *International Journal On Advances in Intelligent Systems* 6, nos. 3–4, pp. 235–55. [Bodendorf, F., (ed.)], ISSN: 1942-2679, LCCN: 2008212456 (Library of Congress), OCLC: 826628364. http:// iariajournals.org/intelligent_ systems/intsys_v6_n34_2013_paged.pdf

Rückemann, C.-P. 2014a. "Knowledge Processing for Geosciences, Volcanology, and Spatial Sciences Employing Universal Classification." In *Proceedings of The Sixth International Conference on Advanced Geographic Information Systems, Applications, and Services (GEOProcessing 2014)*, March 23–27, pp. 76–82. Barcelona, Spain: XPS Press. ISSN: 2308-393X, ISBN: 978-1-61208-326-1. http://thinkmind.org/ download. php?articleid=geoprocessing_2014_4_10_30044

Rückemann, C.-P. 2014b. "Long-term Sustainable Knowledge Classification with Scientific Computing: The Multi-disciplinary View on Natural Sciences and Humanities." *International Journal on Advances in Software* 7, nos. 1–2, pp. 302–17. (ISSN: 1942-2628). http://iariajournals.org/software/soft_v7_ n12_2014_paged.pdf

Rückemann, C.-P. 2014c. "Computing Optimised Result Matrices for the Processing of Objects from Knowledge Resources." In *Proceedings of The Fourth International Conference on Advanced Communications and Computation (INFOCOMP 2014)*, July 20–24, 2014. pp. 156–62. Paris, France: XPS Press. (ISSN: 2308-3484). http://thinkmind.org/download. php?articleid=infocomp_2014_7_20_60039

Rückemann, C.-P. 2015. "Creating Knowledge-based Dynamical Visualisation and Computation." In *Proceedings of the Seventh International Conference on Advanced Geographic Information Systems, Applications, and Services (GEOProcessing 2015)*, February 22–27, pp. 56–62. Lisbon, Portugal: XPS Press. (ISSN: 2308-393X, ISBN: 978-1-61208-383-4). http://thinkmind. org/down load.php?articleid=geo processing_2015_3_40_30063

Rückemann, C.-P., and B.F.S. Gersbeck-Schierholz. 2011. "Object Security and Verification for Integrated Information and Computing Systems." In *Proceedings of the Fifth International Conference on Digital Society (ICDS 2011), Proceedings of the International Conference on Technical and Legal Aspects of the e-Society (CYBERLAWS 2011),* February 23–28. [Berntzen, L., Villafiorita, A., Perry, M. (eds.)] Gosier, Guadeloupe, France: Digital World XPS, Xpert Publishing Solutions. http://thinkmind.org/download. php?articleid=cyberlaws_2011_1_10_70008

Russel, R.C., and M.K. O'Dell. 1918. U.S. patent 1261167. (Soundex algorithm), patent issued 1918-04-02.

SHaRED 2017. *Submission, Harmonisation and Retrieval of Ecological Data (SHaRED).* Retrieved from http://aekos.org.au/SHaRED

SPENVIS (Space Environment Information System). 2017. *The Space Environment Information System (SPENVIS).* Paris, France: The European Space Agency (ESA). https://spenvis.oma.be/

Stok, M. 1994. *Perl, Soundex.pm,* Soundex Perl Port. (code after Donald E. Knuth).

Tcl Developer Site 2017. Tcl Developer Site. Retrieved from http://tcl.tk/

TERN (Terrestrial Ecosystem Research Network). 2017. *Terrestrial Ecosystem Research Network,* Australia, Retrieved from http://tern.org.au

tDAR (The Digital Archaeological Record). 2017. *Digital Archaeological Record,* Retrieved from http://tdar.org

Umweltbundesamt, ed. 1992. *UMPLIS Informations- und Dokumentationssystem Umwelt, Umweltforschungskatalog 1992, (UFOKAT '92).* Erich Schmidt Verlag GmbH & Co., Berlin, 9. Ausgabe, ISBN:3-503-03380-7.

UDCC (Universal Decimal Classification Consortium). 2017. Retrieved from, http://udcc.org

UDCS (Universal Decimal Classification Summary). 2017. *Universal Decimal Classification Summary,* Retrieved from http://udcc.org/udcsummary/php/ index.php

UDCS (Universal Decimal Classification Summary) Translations. 2017. *Universal Decimal Classification Summary (UDCS) Translations,* Retrieved from http:// udcc.org/ udcsummary/translation.htm

UDCS (Universal Decimal Classification Summary). Translations: German. 2017. *Universal Decimal Classification Summary (UDCS) Translations: German.* Retrieved from, http://udcc.org/udcsummary/php/index.php?lang=6

UDCS (Universal Decimal Classification Summary). Exports. 2017. *Universal Decimal Classification Summary (UDCS) Exports,* Retrieved from http://udcc. org/ udcsummary/exports.htm

UDCS (Universal Decimal Classification Summary). Linked Data. 2017. *Universal Decimal Classification Summary (UDCS) Linked Data.* Retrieved from http://udcdata.info

UNEP-GRID. 2017. *United Nations Environment Programme / Global Resource Information Database (UNEP-GRID),* Retrieved from http://grid.unep.ch/ index.php?lang=en

Wesoky, H.L. 1997. "Research Focal Point Report; CO_2, NO_x and Related Topics." In *Contribution to the Committee on Aviation Environmental Protection.* Seville, Spain: ICAO.

Wissenschaftsrat. 2011. *Übergreifende Empfehlungen zu Informationsinfrastrukturen,* (English: Spanning Recommendations for Information Infrastructures), Wissenschaftsrat, Deutschland, (English: Science Council, Germany), Drs. 10466-11, Berlin, 28.01.2011, 2011, Retrieved from http://wissenschaftsrat. de/download/archiv/10466-11.pdf

WDL (World Digital Library). 2017. *World Digital Library,* Retrieved from http://wdl.org

Yin, L., S.L. Shaw, D. Wang, E.A. Carr, M.W. Berry, L.J. Gross, and E.J. Comiskey. 2011. "A Framework of Integrating GIS and Parallel Computing for Spatial Control Problems—A Case Study of Wildfire Control." *International Journal of Geographical Information Science* 26, no. 4, 621–41. doi:10.1080/136588 16.2011.609487

Further Reading

Inden, U., D.T. Meridou, M.E.C. Papadopoulou, A.C.G. Anadiotis, I.S. Venieris, and C.-P. Rückemann. 2014. "Aspects of Modelling and Processing Complex Networks of Operations' Risk." *International Journal on Advances in Software,* ed. L. Lavazza, vol. 7, nos. 3–4, pp. 501–25. ISBN-13: 978-1-63439-815-2, Retrieved from http://thinkmind.org/index.php?view=article&articleid=soft_ v7_n34_2014_7

Leitão, P., U. Inden, and C.-P. Rückemann. 2013. "Parallelising Multi-agent Systems for High Performance Computing." In *Proceedings of The Third International Conference on Advanced Communications and Computation (INFOCOMP 2013)*, November 17–22, pp. 1–6. Lisbon, Portugal: XPS Press. (ISSN: 2308-3484, ISBN-13: 978-1-61208-037-6). http://thinkmind. org/download.php?articleid=infocomp_2013_1_10 _10055

Meridou, D. T., U. Inden, C.-P. Rückemann, C.Z. Patrikakis, D.T.I. Kaklamani, and I.S. Venieris. 2015. "Ontology-based, Multi-agent Support of Production Management." In *The Fifth Symposium on Advanced Computation and Information in Natural and Applied Sciences, Proceedings of the 13th International Conference of Numerical Analysis and Applied Mathematics (ICNAAM)*, September 23-29. Rhodes, Greece, Proceedings of the American Institute of Physics (AIP), AIP Conference Proceedings, volume 1738. AIP Press, American Institute of Physics, Melville, New York, USA, Juni 2016. Simos, T. E., Tsitouras, C. (eds.), ISBN-13: 978-0-7354-1392-4, ISSN: 0094-243X (American Institute of Physics Conference Proceedings, print), DOI: 10.1063/1.4951834.

Rückemann, C.-P. 2016. "Advanced Association Processing and Computation Facilities for Geoscientific and Archaeological Knowledge Resources Components." In *Proceedings of The Eighth International Conference on Advanced Geographic Information Systems, Applications, and Services (GEOProcessing 2016)*, April 24–28, pp. 69–75. Venice, Italy: XPS Press, Rückemann, C.-P., and Y. Doytsher, eds. (ISSN: 2308-393X, ISBN-13: 978-1-61208-469-5). Retrieved from http://thinkmind.org/index.php?view=article &articleid=geoprocessing_2016_4_20_30144

Rückemann, C.-P. 2016. "Enhancement of Knowledge Resources and Discovery by Computation of Content Factors." In *Proceedings of The Sixth International Conference on Advanced Communications and Computation (INFOCOMP 2016)*, May 22–26, 2016. pp. 24–31. Valencia, Spain. XPS Press. [Rückemann, C.-P., Pankowska, M. (eds.)], (ISSN: 2308-3484, ISBN-13: 978-1-61208-478-7). Retrieved from http://thinkmind.org/download. php?articleid=infocomp_2016_2_30_60047

Rückemann, C.-P. 2015. "Cognostics and Knowledge Used With Dynamical Processing." *International Journal on Advances in Software*, ed. L. Lavazza, vol. 8, nos. 3–4, pp. 361–76. ISSN: 1942-2628, LCCN: 2008212462 (Library of Congress). Retrieved from http://iariajournals.org/software/soft_ v8_n34_2015_ paged.pdf

Annexure

Table 3.2 Example for classification references, which can be integrated with the knowledge resources: References based on the Universal Decimal Classification (UDC) provided under creative commons license, used for objects on environment and climatology

Classification	Description text (excerpt, english version)
UDC:3	Social sciences
UDC:349.6	Environmental protection law
UDC:379.84	Outdoor, open-air recreation (according to physical environment)
UDC:5	Mathematics. Natural sciences
UDC:500	Natural sciences
UDC:502/504	Environmental science. Conservation of natural resources. Threats to the environment and protection against ...
UDC:502	The environment and its protection
UDC:502.1	The environment and society. Conservation and protection in general
UDC:502.11	Interaction, interdependence of environment and society. Mutual benefits, etc.
UDC:502.12	Environmental awareness. "Green" outlook. Green issues. "Greenness"
UDC:502.13	Conservation measures and management
UDC:502.131	Development
UDC:502.14	Social, administrative, legislative measures on environmental conservation
UDC:502.15	Environment in relation to planning and development
UDC:502.17	Protection of the environment in general
UDC:502.171	Protection, rational use and renewal of natural resources
UDC:502.174	Restoration, salvage, reclamation, rescue measures. Wasteless and low-waste technology
UDC:502.175	Control of environmental quality. Control of pollution
UDC:502.2	The environment as a whole
UDC:502.21	Natural resources and energy
UDC:502.211	The living world. The biosphere
UDC:502.3	Atmospheric environment
UDC:502.5	Earth's surface. Landscape. Scenery
UDC:502.51	Hydrospheric environment

Classification	Description text (excerpt, english version)
UDC:502.52	Lithospheric environment
UDC:502.6	Glacial environment
UDC:504	Threats to the environment
UDC:504.1	Direct damage. Depredation. Threat of depredation
UDC:504.4	Damage from natural causes. Natural disasters. Natural hazards
UDC:504.5	Damage from harmful materials. Pollution
UDC:504.61	Damage by man to the environment
UDC:504.7	Global warming. "Greenhouse effect"
UDC:51	Mathematics
UDC:510	Fundamental and general considerations of mathematics
UDC:511	Number theory
UDC:512	Algebra
UDC:514	Geometry
UDC:517	Analysis
UDC:519.1	Combinatorial analysis. Graph theory
UDC:519.2	Probability. Mathematical statistics
UDC:519.6	Computational mathematics. Numerical analysis
UDC:519.7	Mathematical cybernetics
UDC:519.8	Operational research (OR): mathematical theories and methods
UDC:52	Astronomy. Astrophysics. Space research. Geodesy
UDC:53	Physics
UDC:531/534	Mechanics
UDC:535	Optics
UDC:536	Heat. Thermodynamics. Statistical physics
UDC:537	Electricity. Magnetism. Electromagnetism
UDC:538.9	Condensed matter physics. Solid state physics
UDC:539	Physical nature of matter
UDC:54	Chemistry. Crystallography. Mineralogy
UDC:542	Practical laboratory chemistry. Preparative and experimental chemistry
UDC:543	Analytical chemistry
UDC:544	Physical chemistry
UDC:546	Inorganic chemistry
UDC:547	Organic chemistry
UDC:548/549	Mineralogical sciences. Crystallography. Mineralogy
UDC:55	Earth Sciences. Geological sciences

Classification	Description text (excerpt, english version)
UDC:550	Earth sciences
UDC:550.2	Geoastronomy. Cosmogony
UDC:550.3	Geophysics
UDC:550.31	Generalities
UDC:550.34	Seismology. Earthquakes in general
UDC:550.38	Terrestrial magnetism (geomagnetism)
UDC:550.4	Geochemistry
UDC:550.42	Occurrence and distribution of chemical elements and their isotopes
UDC:550.424	Migration of chemical elements
UDC:550.47	Biogeochemistry
UDC:550.7	Geobiology. Geological actions of organisms
UDC:550.75	Action of humans
UDC:550.8	Applied geology and geophysics. Geological prospecting and exploration. Interpretation of results
UDC:550.83	Geophysical exploration techniques
UDC:550.93	Geochronology. Geological dating. Determination of absolute geological age
UDC:551	General geology. Meteorology
UDC:551.1	General structure of the Earth
UDC:551.2	Internal geodynamics (endogenous processes)
UDC:551.21	Vulcanicity. Vulcanism. Volcanoes. Eruptive phenomena. Eruptions
UDC:551.23	Fumaroles. Solfataras. Geysers. Hot springs. Mofettes. Carbon dioxide vents. Soffioni
UDC:551.24	Geotectonics
UDC:551.26	Structural-formative zones and geological formations
UDC:551.3	External geodynamics (exogenous processes)
UDC:551.312	Limnic type. Formation by fresh water
UDC:551.32	Glaciology
UDC:551.322	Solid water substance. Ice and snow
UDC:551.324	Land ice. Glaciers
UDC:551.326	Floating ice
UDC:551.35	Marine deposits
UDC:551.4	Geomorphology. Study of the Earth's physical forms
UDC:551.43	Relief forms of the Earth's surface. Landforms. Morphostructures
UDC:551.435	Morphosculptures. Relief forms created by exogenous processes. Dynamic and climatic geomorphology

Classification	Description text (excerpt, english version)
UDC:551.44	Speleology. Caves. Fissures. Underground waters
UDC:551.46	Physical oceanography. Submarine topography. Ocean floor
UDC:551.461	General features. Sea level. Horizontal extent
UDC:551.462	Submarine topography. Sea-floor features
UDC:551.463	Seawater. Physical properties of seawater
UDC:551.465	Structure, dynamics, circulation of the sea
UDC:551.466	Sea waves and tides
UDC:551.5	Meteorology
UDC:551.50	Practical meteorology
UDC:551.51	Physics of the atmosphere. Composition and structure of the atmosphere. Dynamic meteorology
UDC:551.52	Radiation. Temperature
UDC:551.55	Wind and turbulence
UDC:551.57	Aqueous vapour. Hydrometeors
UDC:551.576	Cloud
UDC:551.578	Particular forms of precipitation
UDC:551.581	Theoretical climatology. Climatic zones
UDC:551.582	Climatology of particular places, regions, parts of the Earth
UDC:551.583	Natural variations of climate. Climatic change
UDC:551.584	Mesoclimatology. Microclimatology
UDC:551.585.7	Mountain climates
UDC:551.588	Influence of environment on climate
UDC:551.59	Various phenomena and influences
UDC:551.594	Electrical phenomena in the atmosphere
UDC:551.7	Historical geology. Stratigraphy
UDC:551.8	Palaeogeography
UDC:552.1	Rock characteristics and properties generally. Physical and physicochemical petrology
UDC:552.2	General petrography. Classification of rocks
UDC:552.4	Metamorphic rocks
UDC:552.5	Sedimentary rocks
UDC:552.6	Meteorites
UDC:556	Hydrosphere. Water in general. Hydrology
UDC:556.01	Theory. Principles of research and investigation
UDC:556.04	Observations. Data. Records
UDC:556.06	Hydrological forecasting and forecasts
UDC:556.1	Hydrologic cycle. Properties. Conditions. Global water balance

Classification	Description text (excerpt, english version)
UDC:556.11	Water properties
UDC:556.12	Precipitation, rainfall, snow etc. (as element in the hydrologic cycle)
UDC:556.3	Groundwater hydrology. Geohydrology. Hydrogeology
UDC:556.31	Properties of groundwater
UDC:556.33	Aquifers. Water-bearing strata
UDC:556.34	Groundwater flow. Well hydraulics
UDC:556.51	Drainage basins. Catchment areas. River basins. Watersheds
UDC:556.52	Potamology. River systems
UDC:556.53	Rivers. Streams. Canals
UDC:556.536	Hydrodynamics of rivers. Fluvial hydraulics
UDC:556.546	Estuarine hydraulics and hydrodynamics
UDC:556.55	Limnology. Lakes. Reservoirs. Ponds
UDC:56	Palaeontology
UDC:57	Biological sciences in general
UDC:574.3	Populations and environment
UDC:58	Botany
UDC:581.5	Habits of plants. Plant behaviour. Plant ecology. Plant ethology. The plant and its environment. Bionomics ...
UDC:59	Zoology
UDC:591.5	Animal habits. Animal behaviour. Ecology. Ethology. Animal and environment. Bionomy

Legal Issues and Legal Framework with Regard to Climate Change in the Context of the Maritime Industry in South Asia

Shivani Raswan Pathania and Huong Ha

Introduction

The seas of South Asia have become the central focal point for international concerns because of the increasing number of environmental issues affecting the maritime environment. The consequences of environmental degradation are the results of a tendency of continuously exploiting the natural resources and compromising environmental sustainability (Larkin, Smith, and Wrobel 2016). Sustaining the seas in this dynamic world while attempting to ensure the avoidance of issues of sovereignty and states' rights remains as a critical component of durable international governance in the maritime industry. Current global challenges, especially those due to climate change, have severe consequences on mankind, the fisheries, and coastal tourism which threaten the established order of international maritime governance.

The International Maritime Organization (IMO), established under the charter of the United Nations (UN) in 1948, is the founding body for handling all maritime matters (Buky 2009). The United Nations Convention on the Law of the Sea (UNCLOS) has provided a clear direction and an umbrella for the regulatory framework for maritime governance with an increasing focus on climate change (United Nations 1982). This has been ratified by a number of South Asian member states of the UN (India, Nepal, Sri Lanka, Maldives, Bangladesh, Iran, and Pakistan), though the ratification process is still slow and progressing. In fact, having the responsibility for creating a common regulatory framework, for shipping, IMO has contributed to 59 conventions and protocols. Resultantly, these conventions have laid down a regulatory framework for the safe operations and interaction of commercial shipping vessels with the ports they visit.

This chapter discusses the legal framework, including the UNCLOS, for responding to climate change. It focuses on the development of mitigation and adaptation measures to address climate change-related issues (International Institute for Sustainable Development 2016). Thus, this chapter aims to address the following questions in the context of the maritime industry:

1. What are the issues and challenges associated with climate change faced by the maritime industry in South Asia?
2. What is the current legal framework governing the maritime industry in South Asia with regard to mitigation of and adaptation to the impact of climate change?
3. Is the current legal framework effective globally in preventing irreparable harm to the environment?

To clarify terms, mitigation herein is considered as any induced efforts of the international communities to prevent and deal with the threat posed by climate change (Kahn Ribeiro et al. 2007). On the other hand, adaptation includes the success of all efforts to reduce the adverse effect of climate change on the atmosphere (Burton, Diringer, and Smith 2014).

The chapter is structured into three main parts: (i) an introduction of the issues and challenges faced by the maritime industry, (ii) the legal framework relating to climate change mitigation and adaptation governing the maritime industry, and (iii) the effectiveness of the current legal framework, that is, the contributions of UNCLOS and its role in the preservation of an order and effective international legal system in the maritime industry.

A significant aspect of the chapter is to suggest some measures to strengthen the legal framework for the maritime industry. Undoubtedly, the real threat posed by the warmer oceans and rising sea levels presents one of the biggest challenges to the international maritime industry. The root causes of such an irreparable loss are the emission of too much carbon dioxide (CO_2) and sulphur dioxide (SO_2) from the ever-on engines of the ships and other sources of emissions (Ming et al. 2014). Though there is an international legal regime to deal with this threat, new treaties and conventions are imperative in the battle with climate change to ensure the smooth remedy to a rapidly changing maritime domain.

Issues and Challenges Faced by the Maritime Industry

Asia is the largest continent and with the most population on the earth and spread over different climatic zones. The region is facing significant climatic challenges in its efforts to preserve natural resources. This region is more prone to natural hazards, and there is an increase in the frequency and intensity of unexpected weather conditions, such as tropical cyclones, heat waves, rainfall, prolonged dry spills, thunder storms, snow avalanches in the region (Beker 2008; Amirtahmasebi 2016).

The increasing volume of the shipping through the coastal areas has led to a high level of emissions of carbon dioxide (CO_2) which contributes to 3 percent of all global emissions. CO_2 emissions from shipping has been increased by more than 90 percent since 1990, and the amount of carbon emissions due to shipping activities is expected to triple by 2050 (Dings 2015). This contributes to 18 percent of the 2°C carbon budget by 2050 (Dings 2015). The increase in the temperature is one of the factors contributing to global warming and to the melting of glaciers in the Arctic region. Consequently, the melting of the polar icecaps increases sea levels and the merging of continental boundaries in coastal states.

Another major threat to the maritime environment is from contamination by untreated sewage, discharge of oils, pesticides, hazardous wastes and industrial effluents, and other sea-based activities (UNEP CAR/RCU (2014–2015). The massive shipping accidents in the middle of the sea also threaten the marine life and livelihoods of coastal states. Marine pollution is the major threat to the coastal states of the South Asian countries. This is endangering the regional fishing industry, fragile marine habitats, and coastal tourism (UNEP CAR/RCU (2014–2015). The oil pollution from the ships coming for bunkering in some of the South Asian states, such as India and Bangladesh, is a great challenge (Rekadwad and Khobragade 2016). Among the other causes of the oil pollution may be tank cleaning and the unlawful discharge of bilge water and sludge (UNFCCC 2006). The ship traffic in these areas, especially in the Bay of Bengal, also contributes to the operational discharges. The lack of effective monitoring and surveillance, and the tendency of some ship masters to pump bilge water or clean ships' tanks are some additional concerns in the deep waters of South Asia.

An important problem confronting the countries in South Asia is that some of the countries, such as countries in the Middle East, are the major producers of oil and petroleum (Organization of the Petroleum Exporting Countries 2015). Therefore, the danger is always from seepage as well as accidents during production and transport of oil. Oil pollution is recognized as a major problem in the marine environment, which really needs more international attention (Rekadwad and Khobragade 2016; Thorsell and Leschine 2016). The massive oil usually spills near to the shorelines, but there is not enough time for the cleaning process to totally clear the oil spill. Resultantly, the thick layer of sticky oil is deposited on the surface and any solid that comes in contact with the spilled oil. With such a contamination the plant and rare marine species are exposed to an increased danger of extinction. The total impact on the environment, particularly in South Asian countries, is actually difficult to assess because there are limited and fragmented surveys and research on this area (Kelly and Adger 2000; UNEP 2010).

Significantly, many countries in this South Asia region, such as Nepal, have no adequate resources to tackle the challenges posed by marine pollution and climate change. These developing countries are more vulnerable to the impact of climate change than other developed countries because they have very few resources to adapt to climate change technologically, socially, and financially (United Nations 2007). Such countries need constant assistance and support from the international community to adapt to climate change in terms of national planning and implementation for sustainable development as well as adoption of green techniques.

Overall, the greatest challenge in front of international community is warmer oceans and rising sea levels (Mimura 2013). The focus mainly is on the Arctic which leads to the problem of the water of the world at large. There are actually insufficient bilateral and multilateral conventions in this regard to regulate navigational and exploration rights in the Artic (Keskitalo, Koivurova, and Bankes 2009). Another important issue is the ingress and egress of the ships through this area. Emission of too much hazardous gases leads to melting of the glaciers, resultantly to rising sea levels (Mimura 2013).

Legal Framework Governing the Maritime Industry

In order to respond to international major disasters, climatic changes and marine pollution, countries moved toward internationalization of the law. First, they have tried to harmonize national regulations through various bilateral and multilateral treaties, protocols, agreements, meetings, and negotiations among the leading nations and leading maritime organizations (Rogers 2013). Some of these organizations operated and committed to the tasks for some time and then vanished or were incorporated into other. Subsequently, countries were forced to establish international arraignments and universal rules. Finally, some intergovernmental organizations took over the task "in order to encourage the adoption of international instruments to regulate safety at sea and prevention of pollution from ships" (Rogers 2013, p. 3).

Undoubtedly, UNCLOS is the foundational convention of the maritime industry. So far, no amendment in the UNCLOS was made given evolving dangers from climate change. The extreme and unpredictable weather conditions and the power of the sea itself seemed to be so mighty that for several years, people have thought that nothing could be done to make shipping safer and pollution free (International Maritime Organization 2015a).

Regardless of safety regulations, the UNCLOS is the foundation of which all other arrangements and conventions must adhere to its relevant clauses. There is a very important agenda placed in front of the international communities with regard to climate change-related issues, for example, global warming (Martens and Rotmans 2000). Climate change further poses various conflict scenarios in the maritime industry. Another growing threat to the maritime ecosystem is the oil pollution from ships, especially when the Artic Sea is opened to commercial navigation which means more ships will pass by and more emissions will be released into the seas (The International Tanker Owners Pollution Federation Limited 2013; Chang et al. 2014). Another issue is the effect of the sea level rise on maritime borders and national territories (Young 2000; Buky 2009). In a nutshell, the threat from climate change is complex in nature, which necessitates the international agreement for the maintenance of integrated and consistent regime in the maritime industry.

In terms of law administration, IMO's functions as envisaged in the 1948 Convention are an outcome of the various reviews, revisions, and development in the legal framework for governing the maritime industry.

Prevention of Pollution of the Sea by Oil, 1954 (OILPOL 1954)

The International Convention recognized the possibility of oil pollution which affects the marine environment in the Prevention of Pollution of the Sea by Oil, 1954 (OILPOL 1954) (International Maritime Organization 2015b). The OILPOL 1954 disallows the discard of oily waste "within a certain distance from land and in 'special areas' where the danger to the environment was especially acute" (Gunasekera 2010, p. 23). In 1962, the limits were reviewed and revised in a conference organized by the IMO. In 1965, a subcommittee was established by the IMO and its Maritime Safety Committee to handle issues related to oil pollution (Gunasekera 2010).

1973 International Convention for the Prevention of Pollution from Ships (MARPOL)

Annexure I of the 1973 MARPOL Convention included many clauses from the OILPOL 1954 regarding oil control. Other annexures covered various areas, ranging from chemicals, harmful substances, sewage, garbage discard, and so on (International Maritime Organization 2015a). Annexure I of the MARPOL improved the scope and the scale of the OILPOL. For example, it requires the recipients to continuously monitor oily water discharges and provide rectification in case there are any oil leaking incidents.

Annexure I states the requirements for national governments to comply with regarding provision of shore reception and oil treatment facilities at ports and oil refilled stations. According to Annexure I, more stringent discharge standards are required for a number of special areas, where oil incidents have occurred or may occur, such as the Red Sea and Gulf, the Baltic Seas, and the Mediterranean. Among the important items included in Annexure I is Regulation 13 which enforces that ballast tanks on new tankers with more than 70,000 deadweight tons (dwt) must be segregated to avoid the ballast tanks to be contaminated by oil carriers (International Maritime Organization 2015a).

1978 Conference on Tanker Safety and Pollution Prevention

This conference adopted one of the protocols in the 1973 MARPOL Convention. This aims to regulate tankers in a manner which can reduce the likelihood of them to pollute the seas. Previously, only tankers with more than 70,000 dwt need to segregate ballast tanks. However, the 1978 Protocol requires "all new crude oil tankers of 20,000 dwt and above, and all new product carriers of 30,000 dwt and above" to have segregated ballast tanks (International Maritime Organization 2015b, pp. 24–25). The SOLAS (1978 Protocol to the International Convention for the Safety of Life at Sea) also includes additional measures to enhance the safety of tankers. Some other requirements regarding "steering gear for tankers; stricter requirements for carrying of radar and. Collision avoidance aids"; and stricter conditions for certification are also included in the SOLAS.

Both the 1978 MARPOL and SOLAS Protocols are key enhancements to raise the benchmark and international standards for construction and equipment of tankers to avoid pollution incidents (International Maritime Organization 2015b).

Carriage of Chemicals by Ship

Regulations for carriage of chemicals by ships are included in the SOLAS and the International Convention for the Prevention of Marine Pollution from Ships (this was modified by the MARPOL 1973/1978). According to these Protocols, chemical tankers manufactured after July 1, 1986 must comply with the terms in the International Bulk Chemical Code (IBC Code), that is, to adhere to the requirements of design and construction of ships used to carry hazardous and nonhazardous chemicals (Hänninen and Rytkönen 2006).

Prevention of Pollution by Garbage from Ships

Prevention of Pollution by Garbage from Ships regulations are included in Annexure V of the MARPOL 1973/78. Steamship Insurance Management Services Ltd. (2014) explains that waste and garbage from ships can cause as much marine pollution as oil or chemical spills. One of the most dangerous harms to marine life is plastic. "Fish and marine mammals can in some cases mistake plastics for food and they can also become trapped in plastic ropes, nets, bags and other items–even such innocuous items as the plastic rings used to hold cans of beer and drinks together" (International Maritime Organization 2015c, p. 2). Obviously, a great amount of garbage and waste on beaches come from people, who are tourists, fishermen, or even local residents, litter on the beaches. Yet, it was found that in some particular areas, garbage comes from passing ships since many people conveniently think that the seas can swallow anything being thrown to them (International Maritime Organization 2015c).

Prevention of Pollution by Sewage from Ships

Prevention of Pollution by Sewage from Ships regulations can be found in Annexure IV of the MARPOL. Raw sewage together with rubbish which is discharged into the sea can cause health hazard and water pollution. As explained by Mitropoulos (2010), "sewage can also lead to oxygen depletion and can be an obvious visual pollution in coastal areas—a major problem for countries" relying on tourism industry (p. 15). Sewage discharged into the seas comes from both land and ships which contribute to marine pollution. Annexure IV of the MARPOL regulates the equipment and systems of the ships with regard to the sewage discharge. It also introduces a sample of the "International Sewage Pollution Prevention

Certificate" which is supposed to issue by national shipping authorities to ships passing by their jurisdiction (Mitropoulos 2010).

Reception Facilities

The IMO has acknowledged that the availability of reception facilities is essential for the effective implementation of the MARPOL and other conventions. Thus, the Marine Environment Protection Committee (MEPC) has promoted the MARPOL to member countries and encourages them to discharge their duty regarding provision of proper reception facilities for ships. It is observed that "the policy of 'zero tolerance of illegal discharges from ships' could only be effectively enforced when there were adequate reception facilities in ports" (International Maritime Organization 2015d, p. 2). Such facilities will contribute to reduce waste and hazardous substances to be released freely to the seas.

Prevention of Emission of Obnoxious Gases

Annexure VI of the MARPOL regulates the use and carry of sulphur and control of sulphur emissions. In 2008, the IMO has revised the requirements in Annexure VI on the sulphur content contained in marine fuels. Various options have been proposed to ship owners in order to help them comply with the international regulations. Ship owners can choose to use marine diesels or LNG-fuelled carriers or to fit engines with scrubbers or use green technologies in order to reduce the amount of sulphur emissions (Saul and Chestney 2014).

Undoubtedly, the MARPOL also provides an effective framework to deal with the situations of oil spills. The main problem faced by the developing South Asian countries is corruption and bureaucracy. The government needs to make effective domestic legislation to ensure the national standards adhere to the international standards set by MARPOL. For example, in India, the government needs to comply with the basic standard requirements with the close cooperation of the major oil companies and private companies to meet with the requirements for the reception facilities at the ports. National ports need to comply with the international standards to provide the basic reception facilities to deal with the garbage from the ships that dock in the respective ports. This is an effective step toward the control of marine pollution. However, the developing states are reluctant to comply with these regulations.

Effectiveness of the Current Legal Framework

The aforesaid measures undertaken by the international communities around the world are undoubtedly and significantly aimed at ensuring the prevention of harm to the climate. The awareness regarding the prevention of marine pollution among the shipping interests and countries is somewhere given to them by virtue of effective international regulations, principles, and conventions, to which they themselves are collectively responsible for (Boyle 2000; Brunner and Lynch 2010). Though these measures are not backed by stringent legal sanctions but noncompliance will result in possible sanctions from the other countries (Doelle 2009). The international criticism and some kinds of sanctions against the noncompliant countries suffice for the effective implementation of the international measures. Hence, the call among the nations is coordinated efforts, mitigation, adaptation, and cooperation.

Recently, international shipping has agreed to become the first industry to implement the global CO_2 reduction strategy. The IMO has approved the establishment of an Energy Efficiency Design Index (EEDI) (Office of Transportation and Air Quality 2011). This requires the new ships to adopt a minimum standard of energy efficiency. Though this cannot be considered as a solution because the implementation will take many years to be effective, some of the South Asian nations such as India, Bangladesh, and Pakistan opposed the measures though they were considered to be ineligible to vote, as they are not the parties to Annexure MARPOL VI. Therefore, there was a worldwide implication of adoption of this new standard. Ships built in 2013 will have to meet the minimum standard of energy efficiency, with different standards to the different classes of ships. However, it will take years to get the EEDI start to attain the widespread recognition.

Besides the above-mentioned measures, slow steaming is another measure whereby the speed of the ship is reduced. This is introduced so that ships' engines will not operate at full power, and consequently will use up less fuel and emit less CO_2. The purpose of mandatory speed limits is to generate massive reductions in CO_2 emissions from shipping and to help in tackling air pollution from the ships in coastal and port states (Sanguri 2012).

Climate change and environment degradation has emerged as one of the main agenda items which need urgent attention of international organizations, such as the World Bank, regarding the funding of developing nations which actually are more vulnerable to the challenges. The current systems to manage solid waste on inhabited islands, such as Maldives, are insufficient. Therefore, the World Bank has financed projects which can effectively manage environmental risks to protect the fragile coral reefs and other marine ecosystems (World Bank 2010). The main task of these particular projects is to manage the solid waste in the waters, capacity building for the environment, and the provision of technical support for assessment, monitoring, protection, and management of limited natural resources (Regulation 12, MARPOL IV).

The UNCLOS and the MARPOL remain the main instrument through which maritime regulations are laid down. It also codifies the procedure to be followed for overcoming the disputes and conflicts of law. There is no such provision in the UNCLOS, which prohibits the nations from formulating any new multilateral treaties and conventions to adopt or deal with climate change. Nevertheless, the essential element in the international maritime legal regime requires the stability of the governance and more specifically the international legal regime. Substantial amendments to the UNCLOS or an effective multilateral treaty is required to address any climate change disputes among parties, especially with regard to the issues of substantial rise in sea level. The main reason to look forward to the revision of the UNCLOS is to deal with the complex negotiations with the countries where there is a conflict of law.

In all the maritime matters, the UNCLOS provides a legal framework defining the rights, sovereignty, and liabilities by nations, and it is also the major codified framework of the international maritime industry. However, it appears to be lagging behind under the complex unforeseen challenges of climate change coming forth. Thus, the UNCLOS appears to be inadequate to address complex and unforeseen challenges.

In 2011, the MEPC has enforced international ships to adopt energy efficiency measures which were included in chapter 4 in "Annexure VI of the MARPOL Convention" which introduces "a mandatory EEDI for new ships and the Ship Energy Efficiency Management Plan (SEEMP) for all ships," and an International Energy Efficiency Certificate was also introduced (Karim 2013, pp. 3–4).

Many Asian economies have participated in the policy-making processes. Some countries, such as Bangladesh, Japan, Malaysia, the Republic of Korea, and Singapore have been in favor of the new amendment of the MARPOL Convention (Karim 2015). However, other countries, such as China, Kuwait, and Saudi Arabia have showed concerns about the newly enforced regulation and voted against it (Karim 2013). India has also raised its concerns though it did not have any voting rights due to the fact that it was not a party to Annexure VI of the MARPOL (Karim 2015). The protesting countries argued that the amendments should not be imposed on all countries with different economic conditions because they have seriously affected the "Principle of Common but Differentiated Responsibility, which has always been the cornerstone of international climate change law discourse" (Karim 2013, p. 4). It should be noted that some Asian countries played a key role in the negotiation process of the obligations. For instance, the two emerging economies, China and India, played an active role in negotiating the interest of developing countries in negotiations relating to climate change (Michaelowa and Michaelowa 2011; Karim 2015). Saudi Arabia played the key role as the leader of oil exporting countries (Directorate General for Internal Policies, European Union 2013); whereas Japan was the only negotiator in a developed country in Asia in the process (Karim 2013). Many less developed countries in Asia, which have been much affected by climate change, did not have much say in the negotiations (Karim 2015).

Overall, international conventions and maritime law have been applied to all countries. However, different countries may have different mechanisms to enforce law. Also, different countries may have their own national policies and regulations regarding climate change in the context of the maritime industry as proposed by the United Nations Conference on Trade and Development (2013) that national "adaptation strategies to enhance the resilience of maritime transport systems may vary," that is, countries may adopt different mechanism, including "retreat/relocate, protect and/or accommodate" (p. 14). For example, in January 2016, China introduced "its own emission control zones outside of the IMO framework, surrounding some of its largest ports in the Pearl River Delta, Yangtze River Delta and Bohai Sea" (Lajoie 2016). The Netherlands has tried to "promote quality shipping in conformity with international market trends"; whereas Sweden has used "the inflexibility of the demand for port calls to introduce environmental charges linked to the emission of sulphur and nitrogen oxides" (Michaelowa and Krause 2000, p. 134).

The Way Forward

This chapter has discussed (i) the challenges posed by climate change to the maritime industry, (ii) some key conventions and protocols regulating the maritime industry at the international level, and (iii) the effectiveness of such conventions and protocols.

The threat from climate change is problematic because there is no international consensus regarding how to minimize it. UNCLOS does not lay down how to deal with situations such as rapid change in sea level. The world's economies are preoccupied with the ongoing threat from the climate change; however, it is very important that new arrangements, agreements, and conventions need to be established to ensure a smooth adaptation within a rapidly changing maritime regime. It is essential to remember that these conventions are not made for the sake of making them and in fact, their true implementation is also the necessity of the day.

Besides the review and revision of the UNCLOS and the IMO provisions, the developing nations, especially in South Asia, require a range of technical, operational, and regulatory measures to reverse the trend including the EEDI as well as market-based instruments such as instrument trading. The EEDI has long-term benefits if they are applied as soon as they are introduced. There should be less resistance from the countries for its effective implementation at the earliest possible date. There is a call for stronger international cooperation and coordination to deal with the problem of climate change and the laws and regulations need to reflect the dire importance of the situation.

References

Amirtahmasebi, R. 2016. *Mother Nature and South Asian Cities*. Washington, DC: The World Bank Group. http://blogs.worldbank.org/endpovertyinsouthasia/mother-nature-and-south-asian-cities

Beker, M. 2008. "International Law of the Sea." *The International Lawyer* 42, no. 2, pp. 797–810.

Boyle, A. 2000. "Globalisation and Regionalism in the Protection of the Marine Environment." In *Protecting the Polar Marine Environment*, ed. D. Vidas, 19–33. Cambridge, UK: Cambridge University Press.

Brunner, R., and A. Lynch. 2010. *Adaptive Governance and Climate Change*. Boston, MA: American Meteorological Society Publication.

Buky, M. 2009. "Terrorism, Piracy and Climate Change: Challenges to International Maritime Governance." *Social Alternatives* 28, no. 2, pp. 13–17.

Burton, I., E. Diringer, and J. Smith. 2014. *Adaptation to Climate Change: International Policy Options*. Arlington, VA: Pew Center on Global Climate Change.

Chang, S.E., J. Stone, K. Demes, and M. Piscitelli. 2014. "Consequences of Oil Spills: A Review and Framework for Informing Planning." *Ecology and Society* 19, no. 2, p. 26. http://dx.doi.org/10.5751/ES-06406-190226

Dings, J., ed. 2015. "Transport White Paper: Efficient, Electric, Priced and International." Speech delivered at the European Parliament Transport Committee's Hearing on the White Paper Transport. Brussels.

Directorate General for Internal Policies, European Union. 2013. *The Development of Climate Negotiations in View of Warsaw (COP 19)*. Brussels: European Union.

Doelle, M. 2009. "The Climate Change Regime and the Arctic Region." *Climate Governance in the Arctic Environment & Policy* 50, no. 2, pp. 27–50.

Gunasekera, D.M. 2010. *Civil Liability for Bunker Oil Pollution Damage*. Hamburg: Peter Lang.

Hänninen, S., and J. Rytkönen. 2006. *Transportation of Liquid Bulk Chemicals by Tankers in the Baltic Sea*. Otakaari: VTT Technical Research Centre of Finland.

IISD (International Institute for Sustainable Development). 2016. "Summary of the First Session of the Preparatory Committee on Marine Biodiversity of Areas beyond National Jurisdiction." *Earth Negotiations Bulletin (ENB)* 25, no. 6, pp. 1–21.

IMO (International Maritime Organization). 2015a. *History of Safety at Sea*. London: International Maritime Organization.

IMO (International Maritime Organization). 2015b. *Context*. London: International Maritime Organization.

IMO (International Maritime Organization). 2015c. *Prevention of Pollution by Garbage from Ships*. London: International Maritime Organization.

IMO (International Maritime Organization). 2015d. *Reception Facilities*. London: International Maritime Organization.

Kahn Ribeiro, S., S. Kobayashi, M. Beuthe, J. Gasca, D. Greene, D.S. Lee, Y. Muromachi, P.J. Newton, S. Plotkin, D. Sperling, R. Wit, and P.J. Zhou. 2007. "Transport and its infrastructure." In *Climate Change 2007: Mitigation. Contribution of Working Group III to the Fourth Assessment Report of the Intergovernmental Panel on Climate Change*, eds. B. Metz, O.R. Davidson, P.R. Bosch, R. Dave, and L.A. Meyer. Cambridge, UK and New York, NY: Cambridge University Press.

Karim, M.S. 2013. "IMO Technical and Operational Measures for Reduction of Emissions of Greenhouse Gas from Ships: Perspectives of Asian Countries." Working Paper Series No.032. Singapore: Asia Law Institute.

Karim, M.S. 2015. *Prevention of Pollution of the Marine Environment from Vessels: The Potential and Limits of the International Maritime Organization*. Cham: Springer International Publishing.

Kelly, P.M., and W.N. Adger. 2000. "Theory and Practice in Assessing Vulnerability to Climate Change and Facilitating Adaptation." *Climatic Change* 47, no. 4, pp. 325–52.

Keskitalo, C., T. Koivurova, and N. Bankes. 2009. "Climate Governance in the Arctic: Introduction and Theoretical Framework." *Climate Governance in the Arctic Environment & Policy* 50, no. 1, pp. 1–23.

Lajoie, M. 2016. "Shipping's Dirty Secrets." *China Daily Asia*, May 19.

Larkin, A., T. Smith, and P. Wrobel. 2016. "Shipping in Changing Climates." *Marine Policy* 75, 188–90. doi:10.1016/j.marpol.2016.05.033

Martens, P., and J. Rotmans. 2000. *Climate Change: An Integrated Perspective*. Boston, MA: Kluwer Academic Publishers.

Michaelowa, A., and K. Krause. May/June 2000. "International Maritime Transport and Climate Policy." *Intereconomics* 35, no. 3, pp. 127–36.

Michaelowa, K., and A. Michaelowa. 2011. *India in the International Climate Negotiations: From Traditional Nay-Sayer to Dynamic Broker*. Zurich: Center for Comparative and International Studies (CIS), University of Zurich.

Ming, T., R. de Richter, W. Liu, and S. Caillol. March 2014. "Fighting Global Warming by Climate Engineering: Is the Earth Radiation Management and the Solar Radiation Management Any Option for Fighting Climate Change?" *Renewable and Sustainable Energy Reviews* 31, pp. 792–834.

Mimura, N. 2013. "Sea-Level Rise Caused by Climate Change and its Implications for Society." *Proceedings of the Japan Academy, Series B Physical and Biological Sciences* 89, no. 7, pp. 281–301.

Mitropoulos, E.E. 2010. "IMO: 60 Years in the Service of Shipping." In *Serving the Rule of International Maritime Law: Essays in Honour of Professor David Joseph Attard*, ed. A.N.M. Gutiérrez, 7–21. Oxon: Routledge.

Office of Transportation and Air Quality. 2011. *Adoption of an Energy Efficiency Design Index for International Shipping*. Washington, DC: United States Environmental Protection Agency.

OPEC (Organization of the Petroleum Exporting Countries). 2015. *OPEC Share of World Crude Oil Reserves, 2014*. Vienna, Austria: Organization of the Petroleum Exporting Countries.

Rekadwad, B.N., and C.N. Khobragade. December 2016. "Is the Increase in Oil Pollution a Possibility of the Presence of Diverse Microorganisms? An Experimental Dataset on Oil Prevalent Areas of Goa, India." *Data in Brief* 9, pp. 8–12.

Rogers, A. 2013. "The Evolution of SOLAS." *Shipping & Marine: The Magazine for Maritime Management* 1, online. Norwich: Schofield Publishing Ltd.

Sanguri, M. 2012. *The Guide to Slow Steaming on the Ships*, 18–28. Mumbai, India: Marine Insight Publishers.

Saul, J., and N. Chestney. 2014. "Europe Set for Compliance Chaos with New Ship Fuel Sulphur Rules." *Reuters,* June 20.

Steamship Insurance Management Services Ltd. 2014. *Noxious Liquids in Bulk, Vegetable Oils and Amendments to the IBC Code*. London: Steamship Insurance Management Services Ltd.

The International Tanker Owners Pollution Federation Limited. 2013. *Handbook*, 24–32. London: The International Tanker Owners Pollution Federation Limited.

Thorsell, D.E., and T.M. Leschine. October 2016. "An Evaluation of Oil Pollution Prevention Strategies in the Arctic: A comparison of Canadian and U.S. approaches." *Marine Policy* 72, pp. 255–62.

UNFCCC (United Nations Framework Convention on Climate Change). 2006. *Climate Change: Impacts, Vulnerabilities and Adaptation in Developing Countries*. Bonn, Germany: UNFCCC Secretariat.

UNEP (United Nations Environment Programme). 2010. "Assessing the Environmental Impacts of Consumption and Production: Priority Products and Materials." In *A Report of the Working Group on the Environmental Impacts of Products and Materials to the International Panel for Sustainable Resource Management*, eds. E. Hertwich, E. van der Voet, S. Suh, A. Tukker, M. Huijbregts, P. Kazmierczyk, M. Lenzen, J. McNeely, and Y. Moriguchi. Paris: UNEP.

UNEP CAR/RCU. 2014–2015. *Wastewater, Sewage and Sanitation*. Jamaica: UNEP CAR/RCU.

United Nations. 1982. *United Nations Convention on the Law of the Sea (UNCLOS)*. New York, NY: United Nations.

United Nations. 2007. *Least Developed Countries Most Vulnerable to Climate Change—UN Official*. New York, NY: United Nations. http://un.org/apps/news/story. asp?NewsID=23080

UNCTAD (United Nations Conference on Trade and Development). 2013. *Recent Developments and Trends in International Maritime Transport Affecting Trade of Developing Countries*. Geneva: United Nations Conference on Trade and Development.

World Bank. 2010. *World Development Report 2010: Development and Climate Change*. Washington, DC: World Bank.

Young, O. August 27–29, 2000. "The Structure of Arctic Cooperation: Solving Problems/Seizing Opportunities." Paper prepared at the request of Finland in preparation for the Fourth Conference of Parliamentarians of the Arctic Region, Rovaniemi.

Further Reading

Bueger, C. 2015. "What is Maritime Security?" *Marine Policy* 53, pp. 159–64.

Gormley, K.S.G., A.D. Hull, J.S. Porter, M.C. Bell, and W.G. Sanderson. 2015. "Adaptive Management, International Co-Operation and Planning for Marine Conservation Hotspots in a Changing Climate." *Marine Policy* 53, pp. 54–66.

Lemmen, D.S., F.J. Warren, T.S. James, and C.S.L.M. Clarke, eds. 2016. *Canada's Marine Coasts in a Changing Climate*. Ottawa: Government of Canada.

MacLachlan, S. 2016. *Carbon Emissions All at Sea: Why was Shipping Left Out of the Paris Climate Agreement? OECD Insights Debate the Issues*. Paris: OECD.

Rutherford, V.E., J.M. Hills, and M. Le Tissier. 2016. "Comparative Analysis of Adaptation Strategies for Coastal Climate Change in North West Europe." *Marine Policy* (inpress), http://dx.doi.org/10.1016/j .marpol.2016.07.005i

CHAPTER 5

The Legal Industry Response to Climate Change in Malaysia

Olivia Tan Swee Leng

Introduction

The extensive growth and technology advancements which is brought by industrial revolution are the two tremendous tolls for natural resources (Callen and Thomas 1996). Transport rubbish, manufacturing process, telecommunication, and synthetic chemicals are considered products from essential human consumption and they are the causes of environmental degradation. Science and technology recognizes that there is a trade-off between these two issues, which without each other, there are not enough resources. Developing countries desire their governments to be ethically responsible for the next generation and their citizens to keep the environment safe. Hence, these countries require them to think about the causes of these environmental problems and the solutions to solve them. Human factors have contributed to climate change such as: human built factories, conducting open burning and the use of man-made vehicles, which release harmful gas. The release of large quantities of carbon emission "eats up" the ozone layer. When the ozone layer diminishes, more of the sun's rays enter earth's atmosphere with less restriction and therefore causes the climate to become hotter.

We cannot expect to design a model where the earth has perfectly clean air, 100 percent pure water, nor should we continue to progress economically without respect to the future and the next generation. This scenario is impossible and incites the following questions:

1. What factors play a prominent role in this economic and environmental problem?
2. What level of environment quality is acceptable for countries?
3. How can governments provide a balanced environment and economy with regards to development of the society and market behavior?

In short, which is the best design or plan to adjust environmental policy and better develop the economy?

Environmental Issues

Based on economic theory (Macro Economics), the author analyzed the environmental problems such as the causes and how decision makers are able to solve the problem. In the case of pollution or resource depletion, two categories of today's society (households and firms) have direct responsibility. There are many questions arising here and the answers to them can solve the problems faced by the decision makers. For instance, consumption and production not only need to use resources, but also produce different types of pollution.

There is no person in the world who disagrees with preserving the environment. According to ZhongXiang (2009), there is no decision maker who without analyses of environmental impacts on economics of countries will make any decision. In this case, the direct relationship between environmental policy and economic growth is clear. In developing countries, because of environmental pollution, control policies for (air, water, noise, and mental) pollution increases as well (Andrew 2008; Jaafar, Al-Amin, and Siwar 2008).

As a result of the increased pollution and its global impact, the international agreements, such as the Kyoto Protocol, were initiated by the United Nations (UNFCCC 2014). The Kyoto Protocol is an international agreement between 37 industrialized countries and also European community to protect the climate and especially to prevent the greenhouse gas (GHG) emission. The agreement asked all countries under this agreement to keep the GHG emission amount up to the 5 percent level of 1992 in 2008–2012. In 2015, 196 then parties to the convention came together for the meeting in Paris on November 30–December 12, 2015 and adopted by consensus the Paris Agreement, aimed at limiting global warming to less than 2°C, and pursue efforts to limit the rise to 1.5°C. The Paris Agreement is to be signed in 2016 and will enter into force upon ratification by 55 countries representing over 55 percent of GHG emissions (Paris Convention 2015).

In 1972, the movement to solve the earth's environmental problems began and a conference was set up in Stockholm to find the solution. Subsequent to this conference, the next conference took place 20 years later in 1992 in Rio de Janeiro also known as the Earth Summit. The Rio Conference initiated the start of solving the environmental problems faced by human society. The important product of this conference was the FCCC (Framework Convention on Climate Change), which was signed by 154 countries (Meaken 1992).

The important policies in the FCCC were:

1. Establish a focus on reducing the amount of GHG emission without threats to food production and also any problem for development of countries.
2. Developed countries have to take more serious action to reduce the GHG emission.
3. This agreement is without any GHG reduction aims, timeframes, or any penalties for countries that do not have the means to reduce their GHG emission.
4. All the participants agreed to have regular meetings at the COPs (Conference of the Parties) in order to discuss the follow-up action and other arisen issues.

Following these policies, the Paris Agreement was adopted, which is within the framework of the UNFCCC dealing with GHGs emissions mitigation, adaptation, and finance starting in the year 2020. An agreement on the language of the treaty was negotiated by representatives of 195 countries at the 21st Conference of the Parties of the UNFCCC in Paris and adopted by consensus on December 12, 2015. It was opened for signature on April 22, 2016 (Earth Day) in a ceremony in New York City.

As of September 2016, 180 UNFCCC members have signed the treaty, 26 of which have ratified it, which is not enough for the treaty to enter into force (Paris Agreement 2016).

Prior to the Paris Agreement on Climate Change 2015, in December 1997, the Kyoto Protocol took place after two COPs in Berlin and Geneva. According to the Kyoto Protocol, the members decided to:

1. Provide the table which contain emission target aims reduction for each member of the protocol.
2. Each member should have a GHG emission-trading program (Paris Agreement 2016).

In the Kyoto Protocol, the responsibility and commitment of all countries is not the same. Based on historical data, developed countries are more responsible as in the case of producing GHG. In the recent Paris Agreement 2016, the aim of the convention is described in Article 2, "enhancing the implementation" of the UNFCCC through:

(a) Holding the increase in the global average temperature to well below 2°C above preindustrial levels and to pursue efforts to limit the temperature increase to 1.5°C above preindustrial levels, recognizing that this would significantly reduce the risks and impacts of climate change;
(b) Increasing the ability to adapt to the adverse impacts of climate change and foster climate resilience and low GHG emissions development, in a manner that does not threaten food production;
(c) Making finance flows consistent with a pathway toward low GHG emissions and climate-resilient development.

Countries furthermore aim to reach "global peaking of GHGGHG emissions as soon as possible." The Paris Deal is the world's first comprehensive climate agreement (United States and China announce steps to join the Paris accord that set nation-by-nation targets for cutting carbon emissions, *CBS News, September 3, 2016*).

Control Policies

Control policies are applicable laws, decisions, and regulations authorized by the government to endeavor to prevent any business activities from making pollution for air, water, and total human environment. Control policies are always associated with economic and technological tools of each country.

Subsequent to the industrial revolution and the rise of demand to keep the environment safe, the Malaysia government tried to publish new laws to prevent increasing pollution, such as control policies. Today, there are many alternatives, both legal (carbon and sulphur tax, green tax, energy tax, out-put tax, etc.) and nonlegal instruments, to not only decrease the harmful emission such as carbon dioxide or sulphur dioxide, but also try to keep them at the minimum level (Bolbol, Fatheldin, and Omran 2005). Malaysia is well on track to hit its target of cutting the carbon emissions intensity of the country's GDP by 40 percent by 2020 (*The Sun Daily*, September 24, 2014).

These control policies are aimed to:

- Reduce emission of GHG.
- Reduce waste in all industrial processes.

Unfortunately, because of different abilities of different countries to implement such control policies and also lack of the same interest among countries to follow these control policies, GHG emission abatement targets is still so far from the goal set in the Kyoto Protocol (Matsumoto and Masui 2011; Matsumoto 2007). Malaysia, with a forest land covering 56.4 percent of its territory, is a key player in the global efforts to reduce carbon emissions. The new commitment, however, is subject to technology transfer and new additional funding from developed nations. Malaysia is also among the few developing countries that have met all the eight targets of the Millennium Development Goals, and renewed its commitment to strike a balance between environmental conservation and sustainable development (*New Straits Times* 2013).

Malaysia Economics

Malaysia is a developing country having great growth since the last three decades. The most effective determinants of economic growth of Malaysia are export manufacturing of electronics, crude petroleum, palm oil, and processed timber. This is important when all these manufacturing aspects cause the movement in economic growth of Malaysia.

After the Asian Financial Crisis of 1997–1998, Malaysia's government tried to improve the country's broken economy. Exporting of oil, palm, rubber industries; attempting to be one of the educational cores in Asia; and attracting the attention of tourists to Malaysia are among other ways to improve Malaysia's economy (Deesomsak, Paudyal, and Pescetto 2004). Malaysia's economy improved with growth rates averaging 5.5 percent per year from 2000–2008 (World Bank 2016). In 2009, the Global Financial Crisis affected Malaysia, but the country recovered immediately in 2009 posting growth rates averaging 5.7 percent in 2010 (World Bank 2016).

The Roots of the Problem

Malaysia is one of the countries which improved their economy after the Asian Financial Crisis of 1997–1998. All the macroeconomic variables, such as GDP, unemployment, investment, net export, government expenditure, show that the Malaysian government invested wisely.

Achievement of this goal requires the need to understand all the barriers and limitations. Developed countries are associated with using more resources and particularly those, which produce gas emission (GHG emission). Although economic development is significant for all countries, governments are also concerned with resources and to keep the environment safe and pure (ZhongXiang 2009).

Government and decision makers should bear in mind while they follow the positive profit project, whether they adhere to environmental policy or not. This question forces decision makers to understand the past experiences of countries, such as implementation of carbon taxes and also recognize the barriers and opportunities when they ignore or accept any project.

This chapter attempts to analyze the limitation and problems faced by the decision makers in Malaysia to implement certain policies to manage climate change and the impact of such policies on the economy of Malaysia.

Addressing the Questions and Objectives of Climate Change in Malaysia

Implementing certain policies such as carbon tax for each country needs understanding of economic situations, social situations, and lifestyle of the people. As stated and explained in the afore-mentioned articles, any tax can be disadvantageous for people and particularly for the middle class and the poor. Therefore, there are two questions to address:

1. What are the measures taken by the legal sector and professionals to manage the intense climate change in Malaysia?
2. How do the global issues and policies affect the economic growth in Malaysia?

Human commitment to the environment is required for keeping the environment safe for the next generation. Decision makers should take note about the sensitivity of any threat for human life, food and also energy despite the fact that, keeping the environment safe for humans is one of the significant things. These policies must not affect food or threaten the lifestyle of the people.

In this case, the objective of this chapter is:

1. To examine policies taken by the government of Malaysia to manage the intense climate change.
2. To analyze to what extent such issues and policies affect the growth of economy in Malaysia.

This chapter can assist the government of Malaysia in decision making for human life, the economy, and also the environment. Climate change plays a prominent role in the lifestyle of a household, and also climate change affects the credibility and economy of the country. The economic importance is that climate change affects the export and import of countries around the world. As for society, the importance is because any policy such as carbon tax imposed will have significant effect on the country. All these reasons mentioned earlier makes this chapter significant for the government, legal industries, and cooperation among other members of society in responding to the climate change issues.

Malaysia's international trade has a significant role in boosting the economy of Malaysia. Malaysia is one of the third largest producers of tin, rubber, and also palm oil in the world. Manufacturing firms contribute to the growing economy of the country. Malaysia's banking system is also the largest Islamic and financial system in the world.

The result of the progress described, leads to consumption of more energy and particularly fossil fuels. Based on the referred literature, there is a direct link between consuming energy (high intensive Carbon Producer) and also the economic development of one country. In this case, Malaysia becoming an industrialized country and at the same time keeping the earth clean with environmental policies, has become a pertinent study in this chapter.

Effect of Carbon Taxes and Environmental Policies

Several articles as stated below show that any tax such as carbon tax and all other environmental policies will affect the macroeconomic variable. The degree of differences of their effect is completely different. For instance, GDP reduces by implementing carbon tax, but carbon tax effects GDP for each country differently.

The government of Malaysia should strike a balance between the degree of pressure, which is imposed by implementing any policy to curb climate change to middle and low-income households. If implementation is done without considering its effect on the society, it can cause many problems, in particular for the poor families.

Lin and Li (2011) analyzed 17 countries of EU (Denmark, Finland, Sweden, Netherlands, Austria, Belgium, Czech Republic, France, Greece, Hungary, Iceland, Ireland, Luxembourg, Poland, Portugal, Slovakia, Spain, and Norway). For their measurement, they provided data from

1981 to 2008. In their methodology, they used Panel Data regression because of the great amount of data (Time and Variable). The author also mentioned that, in comparison with others, they used DID (difference in difference) because in previous studies they were more focused on the theoretical section of carbon tax, but this article is more focused on real mitigation of carbon tax. After their investigation, they found that the increase in GDP per capita is positively related with increase of CO_2 emission, which means increase in GDP has a sharp and positive effect on CO_2 emission. The second result indicates that urbanization does have significant effect on CO_2 emission. The last result of this study shows that effect of carbon tax in different countries is completely different because of different carbon tax rates in these countries and different levels of tax exemption and different usage of carbon tax revenue (Lin and Li 2011).

Shree Raj Shakya, Kumar, and Shrestha (2011) analyzed the effect of carbon tax on a country utilizing hydropower, such as Nepal. Their sample size was between 2005 and 2050. In their analyses, they attempted to determine the relationship between carbon tax with energy mix, environmental emissions energy supply security, energy efficiency, energy system cost, and employment benefit. After their investigation, they proved that increase in carbon tax (\$13 per CO_2 in 2015 to \$50 per CO_2 in 2050) causes reduction in amount of emission of GHGs. They mentioned that local pollutants (SO_2, NO_x, NMVOC) were reduced by applying the carbon tax policy in 2050. In the case of imported energy, they show the negative relationship, which means applying the carbon tax policy caused reduction in imported energy. For the last policy, they showed that carbon tax caused increase in new generation of employment, which is associated with hydropower requirement (Shakya, Kumar, and Shrestha 2011).

Wang et al. (2011) analyzed the impact of carbon tax on competitiveness of China's sector in the short term. The reasons for using short-term data is because of carbon tax's effect on a short-term variable could be different and also short-term analyses can complete the accuracy of long term for computing the carbon tax impact on the economy. This study contained 36 sectors; from those the important ones are electricity and heat, ferrous metal, gas production, and textile, among other sectors. Data for this study were for input-output table from 2007. There are two assumptions here. The first one assumes that from the entire merchandise which import, there is no carbon tax for them instead of fossil fuel. The second assumption is for export goods there is no refund of carbon tax. As a result for this study, the author mentioned that electricity and heat are the most affected sectors by carbon tax, but because of the absence of foreign firms, competitiveness is not as high as expected. The short-term effect of carbon tax on imports is not significant. In China, because most of the export products are the final goods, therefore competitive effects of carbon tax decrease. From other results, the study indicates that if carbon tax is low, competitiveness effect is not important. From another view, if carbon tax is high, each sector needs to use compensatory measure, and also in this competitiveness effect is high. One of the limitations were the non-existing CO_2 emission statistical data, which forced the author to use the sectoral total energy consumption data. The second problem was because of absence of data, they ignored to use industrial process emission.

Zhao (2011) investigated the effect of carbon tax on the world's competitiveness between OECD (Organization for Economic Cooperation and Development) countries during 1992–2008. The countries among this sample size are: Austria, Australia, Belgium, Canada, Denmark, Finland, France, Germany, Greece, Ireland, Italy, Japan, Netherlands, New Zealand, Norway, Hungry, Spain, Sweden, Switzerland, United Kingdom, and the United States. The first question by the author is their reasons to choose OECD countries as their sample size. First of all, these countries implement the carbon tax, therefore all the data are available for the authors. Second, there are many factors which affect the competitiveness of countries besides carbon tax in these countries, such as labor, political stability, and technology, among others. However, quantitative measure of these factors is not easy and the benefit of choosing these countries is that they are close to each other in all these cases. These countries also have an energy price system. Therefore, the countries' variables except carbon tax are the same or close to each other and the effects are negligible. As their method in this study they use two models, which are gravity model and panel data regression method. Competitiveness in industries of each country is measured by share of international market and profitability. In this case, increase in share brings more intensive competitiveness. They indicate that when only the imported countries implement carbon tax, it has negative effect on resource-based industries and non resource-based industries. These countries have strict tariffs, which impose the high price to all energy intensive products. The control policy of environment is strict and it causes these countries to change the location of their factories to another country, where there is no commitment on carbon tax. As a result of this study, the author shows that competitiveness of these countries makes a problem for their export. Because of the increase of price due to carbon tariffs, it causes weakness in their competitive advantage, Zhao mentions that if both imported and exported countries implement the control policy (carbon tax) it offsets their effect (Zhao 2011).

Massetti (2011) tried to design a target emission for China and India, both of which are industrial countries. They indicate that increase in carbon tax from \$10 per ton of CO_2, in India has better effect in GHG because of 30 percent reduction in CO_2 emission. Although they show that emission of GHG increased in India, China still is among the top countries, which produce the most CO_2 in the world.

Hwang (2011) investigated emission reduction in Taiwan. This study was conducted from 1990 to 2007. After his investigation, he announced that Taiwan maintained its economic growth by using variety (renewable, coal, petroleum, hydropower, natural gas). He also explained that in Taiwan, energy consumption and GDP has a positive relationship with each other. Among energy, industrial, transportation, agricultural service, and the residential sectors, the industry sector consumes the highest energy. The main issues for reducing GHG are twofold. The first of these issues is that there is no blueprint to reducing greenhouse emission because the regulations are new for preventing carbon dioxide. The second issue is limitation of tools (joint implementation, clean development mechanism, emission trade) in reducing GHG emission. The important part of this study shows that because of not having economies of scale for using clean technology, investors do not choose to invest in clean and friendly environment technology (Hwang 2011).

Matsumoto and Masuri (2011) analyzed the long-term impact of carbon tax on the environment and economy. They used AIM and CGE models to measure their works. After their investigation, they announced that CO_2 abatement between the two different types of taxes, CCT (Common Carbon Tax) and ICT (International Carbon Tax), is almost the same. They indicated that although two different taxes have almost the same result, the economic impact result of such policies is different. They showed that the negative impact of CCT between developed countries is small, but in the case of ICT, the negative impact between developing countries is small. Their findings show that because of worldwide introduction of CO_2 and also decreasing the border of developing countries to implement the carbon tax policies, ICT is more flexible than CCT (Matsumoto and Masui 2011).

Table 5.1 refers to other authors' findings on analyses that affected carbon tax in the respective countries.

Table 5.1 Other authors' findings

Author	Year	Focus	Findings
Lin and Li	2011	European countries	• GDP is positively related to emission of carbon and GHG emission. • Urbanization does not have any significant effect.
Shree Raj Shakya, Kumar, and Shrestha	2011	The effect of carbon tax	• Carbon tax causes reduction in imported energy. • Carbon tax can make new job opportunities for industries which is related to low carbon production such as using hydropower.
Wang et al.	2011	Impact of carbon tax on competitiveness of China's sector in short term	• Short-term result of carbon tax is not significant. • Low rate of carbon tax does not have significant effect on competitiveness of companies.
Hwang	2011	Investigates the different alternative ways to reduce GHG emission in Taiwan	• In Taiwan energy consumption and GDP have a positive relationship with each other. • Between all the sectors (industry, transportation, household, and service, among others), industry and manufacturing have the first rank for consuming of energy.
Masseti	2011	Consider to design an essential model for China and India, to mitigate their emission	• Change in carbon tax rate has better effect on carbon emission in India. • They show that, although China tries to prevent carbon emissions action, it is still the highest carbon producer in the world.

Zhao	2011	Investigate the effect of carbon tax on a world competitiveness between OECD	• Carbon tax can cause difficulties for exporting of these countries. • If both import and export countries implement carbon tax, it is nice for both of them, and offsets any negative effect for exporting countries.

Environmental Policies and Framework

The articles from the year 2011 to 2012 are relevant for the government of Malaysia to refer to when implementing policies in response to tackle climate change issues in the country. The more recent literature review will be discussed on the government's responses or actions taken for this matter. Based on this, a theoretical framework is designed for easy reference (Figure 5.1).

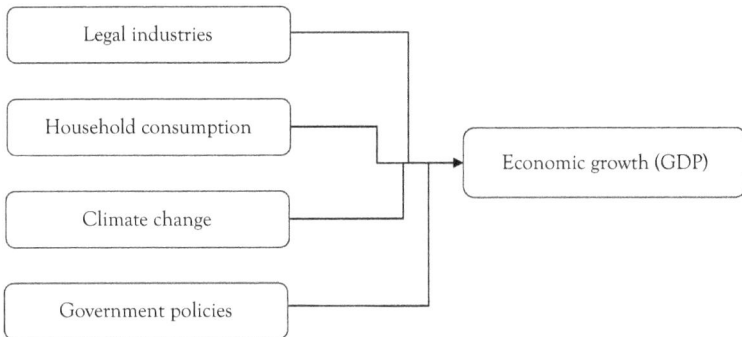

Figure 5.1 Policies framework that contributed to economic growth
Source: Leng

Approaches to Examine Climate Change and the Legal Industry

The study in this chapter is a social-legal case study on the legal industry response to climate change in Malaysia. The author opted for a qualitative research approach and made analyses based on documented materials, books, journals, online materials, field work via interviews, and observations via legal industry response to climate change in Malaysia. The author used case study design to understand thoroughly the issue of climate change in Malaysia. The in-depth understanding of legal industry response to climate change is an end in itself to establish the causes and implication of climate change response in Malaysia.

These methods are used to study some of the significant aspects in the field of climate change and legal industry response such as:

1. Malaysia's experiences of climate change and legal industry response
2. The International laws and instruments and Malaysian laws application and practice on climate change
3. The enforcement of environmental laws and regulations
4. Exploration of other countries' legal jurisdictions such as United States and other regional countries

The author uses case study design to draw data from selected legal industries that are the gate keepers or organization administrators for climate change in Malaysia such as legal industry factories or corporations situated in Malaysia and the climate change steering committees in Malaysia as stated below.

Table 5.2 Organization administrators for climate change in Malaysia

Membership of National Steering Committee on Climate Change. Secretary General, Ministry of Natural Resources and Environment (NRE)–Chairman Conservation and Environmental Management Division, NRE–Secretariat
Malaysian Meteorological Service
Ministry of Energy Water and Communications
Ministry of Plantation Industries Commodities
Ministry of Finance
Ministry of Education Ministry of International Trade and Industry
Ministry of Agriculture Ministry of Foreign Affairs Economic Planning Unit
Attorney General's Office

At present, climate change-related concerns are addressed through various sectors such as energy, forestry and natural resource management, land-use planning, agriculture, solid waste, and drainage and irrigation. Often, actions taken in the realm of "climate change" are guided by Malaysia's international obligations and commitments, namely three conventions:

1. United Nations Framework Convention on Climate Change (UNFCCC),
2. United Nations Convention on Biological Diversity (CBD), and
3. United Nations Convention to Combat Desertification (CCD).

In 1994, the National Steering Committee on Climate Change (NSCCC) was established under the Ministry of Science, Technology and the Environment (MoSTE). Subsequently, the Ministry of Natural Resources and Environment (NRE) was established on March 27, 2004, following the formation of a new cabinet by the prime minister. Note that the secretary general of the NRE chairs the NSCCC, which also acts as the focal point for the UNFCCC.

Policies and Regulations Addressing Climate Change in Malaysia

For Malaysia, climate change is cross-sectoral in nature, involving more than merely environmental issues, but also affecting economic growth and human well-being (Pereira and Subramaniam 2007). For example, the conservation of natural resources and biological diversity is carried out through the implementation of various sectoral laws and regulations such as the *Protection of Wildlife Act* (1972), *Environmental Quality Act* (1974), *Scoping Assessment on Climate Change Adaptation National Forestry Act* (1984), and *Fisheries Act* (1985). The conservation of biodiversity is also addressed in the five-year Malaysia Plan, as well as policies such as the National Policy on Biological Diversity (1998), National Policy on the Environment (2002), National Wetlands Policy (2004), National Physical Plan (2005), and National Urbanisation Plan (2006). These and sectoral laws and regulations have provided a foundation on which climate change relation policies and regulations could support sectoral actions.

Climate Change Projection Programs

Malaysia government has conducted several programs and activities to study the impact on climate change in Malaysia, the "Study of the Impact of Climate Change on the Hydrologic Regime and Water Resources in Sabah and Sarawak (2007–2010)"; the development of the Hydro-Climate Projection Downscaling for Malaysia Using Hadley Centre PRE-CIS Model (2009–2010); and the extension of research on the Impact of Climate Change on the Malaysian Water Resources (2011–2015).

Water resources program includes Integrated Flood Management Program for Pahang and Muar River Basin in Peninsular Malaysia; updating the Integrated Development Plan (IDP) relationship to maintain design standards; integrated rainfall and flood forecasting, warning and response system for Johor, Pahang, Kelantan River Basin which aims to increase lead time forecast to 72 hours and reduce any severe flood impact; The formulation of the climate change impact on design flood; development of a National Water Resources Policy and Law in Malaysia; and the Sarawak Integrated Water Resources Master Plan (mid-2010).

In 2008, Malaysia adopted the climate change policy and the key features of the policy are:

1. Strong use of market-based instruments to develop global price for GHG emissions.
2. Integration of climate change objectives in relevant policies, such as energy, transport, forest, agriculture, and environment.
3. Expedite technological innovation and diffusion.

The key policy instruments for this matter are:

1. Carbon or energy taxes
2. Removal of environmentally harmful subsidies
3. Tradable permit schemes
4. Project-based flexibility mechanisms of the Kyoto Protocol

Despite the activities and programs stated earlier, Malaysia is far behind in the adaptation of the policies and in particular in measures taken to protect its land, water, and coastal resources. This is critical, as the first cost of climate change is often born through floods, droughts, extreme weather events, and of course sea level rises among many other impacts. In part, the reasons for inadequate adaptation measures often result from the lack of awareness, insufficient information and knowledge on the detail of the impact of climate change, and uncoordinated and unilateral management of the individual subsectors. Yet, positive action has begun, for example, the recent UN Climate Summit in New York on September 23, 2014, whereby Datuk Seri Najib Tun Razak, the Prime Minister of Malaysia has recently reiterated Malaysia's commitment toward reducing its carbon intensity by 40 percent by 2020.

The prime minister informed that Malaysia is meeting its targets to reduce its carbon emission intensity of its GDP by 40 percent by 2020, compared to its 2005 levels. The target was originally declared by Malaysia during the United Nations Climate Change Conference 2009 in Copenhagen, Denmark, conditional to receiving assistance in the form of technology transfer and financing from developed countries (UN Climate Summit 2014).

Recent policy changes have reflected Malaysia's commitments toward the carbon emissions reduction pledge. In 2011, the introduction of the *Renewable Energy Act*, through its incentives (such as the improved Feed in Tariff [FiT] rates for renewable energy producers) and the Green Technology Financing Scheme (GTFS) enabling financial assistance has boosted the development of the local renewable energy industry.

The Malaysian palm oil industry plays a vital role in meeting the 40 percent reduction target. Oil palm, with just over 5 million hectares planted in Malaysia is the country's second largest CO_2 sink (after its permanent forest reserves) that absorb 80 mt of CO_2 from our atmosphere. Its biomass, comprising empty fruit bunches, fronds, and so on, is still largely untapped at the moment and have the potential to generate more than 1,300 MW of renewable energy per year through the combustion of palm biomass in power plants and methane capture facilities at the mills.

Conclusions and Recommendations

As mentioned in previous sections, much of Malaysia's efforts in building climate change adaptation knowledge is centered on learning "what Malaysia is adapting to," that is, the condition, whereas how to adapt has for the most part taken second stage. There is no doubt that Malaysia has the base knowledge and capacity needed to begin mainstreaming climate change adaptation within its development framework, as mentioned in the activities and programs created by the government, yet, complacency toward real actions on the ground are very evident. This could well be Malaysia's number one challenge in relation to climate change adaptation. Malaysia's environmental sustainability efforts are robust; yet they only address the environmental change threat and not specifically the climate change threat. This is of concern for numerous living animals and humans within very climate sensitive habitats, that is, climate variations may exceed environmental thresholds where habitats and ecosystems could not recover to existing equilibrium and stable conditions.

This situation is not unique to Malaysia and a change that many countries will have to accept. Reflecting a little on the water resources sector in Malaysia, actions within exemplify points of integration and knowledge building, thus setting the direction for national cooperation and problem solving on climate change adaptation—a shared responsibility among the ministries. Conversely, considering agriculture, in action toward adaptation is largely driven by the presence of unknown future factors or knowledge needed to devise climate change adaptation responses economically and efficiently, at the least, prepare the sector for some degree of productivity losses. These unknowns range from understanding the past climate record with confidence, to local policy issues on micro-scales, for example, rural livelihoods and how "localized adaptation" can be engaged to reduce vulnerabilities respective of small farm holdings—key to food security among the most vulnerable to climate change and climate variability.

Unfortunately, there is no perfect framework for Malaysia, and for some time, expected is that climate change adaptation will remain in a reactive mode rather than proactive. Policy making and the climate change steering committees for climate change adaptation is heavily dependent upon external assistance, and in many cases, building adaptive capacities involve dealing with uncertainties. The uncertainties have strong implications on both national and local level policy development and vis-à-vis, the government policies such as implementation of carbon tax to curb carbon emission on some legal industry and the response from the legal industry to climate change. No doubt this is positively received by many legal industries such as some renown housing developers, yet this remains as evident as the current plunge of global oil price may affect the environment sustainability and corporate responsibilities in the long run. Another recent climate change effect was the flash flood in the states of Perak, Pahang, Terengganu, and Kelantan (2014–2015). The East Coast (Pantai Timur) floods in Malaysia showed a number of evacuees on the rise. The Star (2014) on December 28, 2014, stated that the number of evacuees was up by more than 40,000 to over 160,000 as the floods worsened due to bad weather. In February 2016, *The Strait Times Online* reported that Melaka Tengah district had the highest number of flood victims with 1,530, followed by Alor Gajah (1,480 victims) and Jasin (82 victims).

In view of this, it is further suggested that Malaysia must adopt the climate change policies rather than just depend on external assistance. A proactive role is pertinent here rather than a reactive role. Mother Nature compromises with no man. Malaysia must ensure that the adopted climate change policy in year 2008 and the key features of the policy such as the following are to be implemented:

1. Strong use of market-based instruments to develop global price for GHG emissions.
2. Integration of CC objectives in relevant policies, such as energy, transport, forest, agriculture, and environment.
3. Expedite technological innovation and diffusion.

Malaysia has forwarded its climate change action plan to the United Nations for the UN Climate Change Conference (COP21) in Paris in November 2015. In a document hosted on the UN website, the plan said Malaysia planned to reduce GHG emissions intensity by 45 percent by 2030. The document can be viewed on the UN's Framework Convention on Climate Change website (http://newsroom.unfccc.int/).

References

Baede, A.P.M, ed. 2015. *Annex I. Glossary: IPCC – Intergovernmental Panel on Climate Change. Intergovernmental Panel on Climate Change*, 942. Retrieved from https://ipcc.ch/publications_and_data/publications_and_data_glossary.shtml

Bolbol, A.A., A. Fatheldin, and M.M. Omran. 2005. "Financial Development, Structure, and Economic Growth: The Case of Egypt, (1974–2002)." *Research in International Business and Finance* 19**,** no. 1, pp. 171–94.

Callen, S.J., and J.M. Thomas. 1996. *Environmental Economics and Management: Theory, Policy, and Applications.* Chicago: Irwin.

Deesomsak, R., K. Paudyal, and G. Pescetto. 2004. "The Determinants of Capital Structure: Evidence from the Asia Pacific Region." *Journal of Multinational Financial Management* 14, nos. 4–5, pp. 387–405.

Hwang, J.J. 2011. "Policy Review of Greenhouse Gas Emission Reduction in Taiwan." *Renewable and Sustainable Energy Reviews* 15, no. 2, pp. 1392–402.

Jaafar, A.H., A.Q. Al-Amin, and C. Siwar. 2008. "A CGE Analyses of the Economic Impact of Output-Specific Carbon Tax on the Malaysian Economy." https://mpra.ub.uni-muenchen.de/10210/1/MPRA_paper_10210.pdf

Lin, B., and X. Li. 2011. "The Effect of Carbon Tax on Per Capita CO2 Emissions." *Energy Policy* 39, no. 9, pp. 5137–46.

MPOC (Malaysian Palm Oil Council). 2014. *Malaysia Palm Oil – Enriching Lives.* http://toshakhana32.rssing.com/chan-15917382/latest.php (19th November 2017)

Massetti, E. 2011. "Carbon Tax Scenarios for China and India: Exploring Politically Feasible Mitigation Goals." *International Environmental Agreements: Politics, Law and Economics* 11, no. 3, 209–27.

Matsumoto, K. 2007. *A Study on the International Climate Change Policy for the Post-Kyoto Protocol* [PhD thesis]. Hyogo: Kwansei Gakuin University.

Matsumoto, K., and T. Matsui. 2011. "Analyzing Long-Term Impacts of Carbon Tax Based on the Imuted Price, Applying the AIM/CGE Model." *Management of Environmental Quality: An International Journal* 22, no. 1, pp. 33–47.

Shakya, S.R., S. Kumar, and R.M. Shrestha. 2011. "Co-Benefits of a Carbon Tax in Nepal." *Mitigation and Adaptation Strategies for Global Change*, 17, no. 1, pp. 77–101.

Zhao, Y.H. 2011. "The Study of Effect of Carbon Tax on the International Competitiveness of Energy-intensive Industries: An Empirical Analyses of OECD 21 Countries, 1992–2008." *Energy Procedia* 5, pp. 1291–302.

ZhongXiang, Z. 2009. "An Economic Model-Based Analyses of Climate and Energy Policy." *Journal of Policy Modeling* 31, no. 3, pp. 359–61.

UNFCCC (United Nations Framework Convention on Climate Change). 2014. *Kyoto Protocol.* http://unfccc.int/kyoto_protocol/items/2830.php

Further Reading

Aasness, J., T. Bye, and H.T. Mysen. 1996. "Welfare Effects of Emission Taxes in Norway." *Energy Economics* 18, no. 4, pp. 335–46.

Allsopp, V. 1995. *Understanding Economics.* London and New York, NY: Routledge.

Andrés, A.R., and R.K. Goel. 2012. "Does Software Piracy Affect Economic Growth? Evidence Across Countries." *Journal of Policy Modeling* 34, no. 2, pp. 284–95.

Andrew, P. 2008. *Four Kind of Pollution, Why Riding a Bie Makes Green Sense* [Online].

Bach, S., M. Kohlhaas, and B. Praetorius. 1994. "Ecological Tax Reform Even if Germany has to Go it Alone." *Economic Bulletin* 31, no. 7, pp. 3–10.

Baranzini, A., J. Goldemberg, and S. Speck. 2000. "A Future for Carbon Taxes." *Ecological Economics* 32, no. 3, pp. 395–412.

Barker, T. 1995. "Taxing Pollution Instead of Employment: Greenhouse Gas Abatement Through Fiscal Policy in the UK." *Energy & Environment* 6, no. 1, pp. 1–29.

Barnes, P., and M. Breslow. 2003. "The Sky Trust: The Battle for Atmospheric Scarcity Rent." In *Natural Assets: Democratizing Environmental Ownership*, eds. K. James and B.G. Shelley, 135–49. Washington, DC: Island Press.

Bruvoll, A., and B.M. Larsen. 2004. "Greenhouse Gas Emissions in Norway: Do Carbon Taxes Work?" *Energy Policy* 32, no. 4, pp. 493–505.

Conefrey, T., J.F. Gerald, L.M. Valeri, and R.S.J. Tol. 2008. "The Impact of a Carbon Tax on Economic Growth and Carbon Dioxide Emissions in Ireland." Working Papers WP251. Dublin: Economic and Social Research Institute (ESRI).

Held, S., C. Roger, and N. Eva-Maria, eds. 2013. *Climate Governance in the Developing*. Oxford: Polity Press.

Eiichi, E. 2007. "Market Penetration Analyses of Fuel Cell Vehicles in Japan by Using the Energy System Model MARKAL." *International Journal of Hydrogen Energy* 32, nos. 10–11, pp. 1347–54.

Floros, N., and A. Vlachou. 2005. "Energy Demand and Energy-Related CO_2 Emissions in Greek Manufacturing: Assessing the Impact of a Carbon Tax." *Energy Economics* 27, no. 3, pp. 387–413.

Fong, W.K., H. Matsumoto, C.S. Ho, and Y.F. Lun. 2008. "Energy Consumption and Carbon Dioxide Emission Considerations in the Urban Planning Process in Malaysia." *Journal of the Malaysian Institute of Planners* 6, no. 1, pp. 101–30.

Goto, N. 1995. "Macroeconomic and Sectoral Impacts of Carbon Taxation: A Case for the Japanese Economy." *Energy Economics* 17, no. 4, pp. 277–92.

Goulder, L.H. 1994. "Effects of Carbon Tax in Economy with Prior Tax Distortion: An Intertemporal General Equilibrium Analyses." *Journal of Enviromental Economics and Managments* 29, no. 3, pp. 271–97.

Goulder, L.H. 1995. "Environmental Taxation and the Double Dividend: A Reader's Guide." *International Tax and Public Finance* 2, no. 2, pp. 157–83.

Gujarati, D.N. 1995. *Basic Econometrics*, 3rd ed. New York, NY: McGraw-Hill.

Gujarati, D.N. 2003. *Basic Econometrics.* New York, NY: McGraw-Hill.

Gujarati, D.N. 2004. *Econometrics.* New York, NY: McGraw-Hill.

Hassan, M.K., B. Sanchez, and J.S. Yu. 2011. "Financial Development and Economic Growth: New Evidence from Panel Data." *The Quarterly Review of Economics and Finance* 51, no. 1, pp. 88–104.

Hollo, E., K. Kulovesi, and M. Mehling, eds. 2013. *Climate Change and the Law.* Netherlands: Springer.

Horace H. 2012. *Living in a Law-Carbon Society in 2050.* London: Palgrave Macmilian.

Hyder, P. 2008. "Recycling Revenue from an International Carbon Tax to Fund an Integrated Investment Programme in Sustainable Energy and Poverty Reduction." *Global Environmental Change* 18, no. 3, pp. 521–38.

Jeong, S.J., K.S. Kim, J.W. Park, D.S. Lim, and S.M. Lee. 2008. "Economic Comparison between Coal-Fired and Liquefied Natural Gas Combined Cycle Power Plants Considering Carbon Tax: Korean Case." *Energy* 33, no. 8, pp. 1320–30.

Kuznets, S. 1934a. *Gross Capital Formation, (1919–1933).* Cambridge: National bureau of Economic Research (NBER).

Kuznets, S. 1934b. *National Income, (1929–1932).* Cambridge: National bureau of Economic Research (NBER).

Kwiatkowski, D., P.C.B. Phillips, and P.S.A.Y. Shin. 1992. "Testing the Null Hypothesis of Stationry Against the Alternative of a Unit Root." *Journal for Econometrics* 54, nos. 1–3, pp. 159–78.

Kulovesi, K., and K. Keinänen. 2006. "Long-Term Climate Policy: International Legal Aspects of Sector-Based Approaches." *Climate Policy*, 6, no. 3, pp. 313–25.

Lee, C.F., S.J. Lin, and C. Lewis. 2008. "Analyses of the Impacts of Combining Carbon Taxation and Emission Trading on Different Industry Sectors." *Energy Policy* 36, no. 2, pp. 722–29.

Lee, C.F., S.J. Lin, C. Lewis, and Y.F. Chang. 2007. "Effects of Carbon Taxes on Different Industries by Fuzzy Goal Programming: A Case Study of the Petrochemical-Related Industries, Taiwan." *Energy Policy* 35, no. 8, pp. 4051–58.

Levin, T., V.M. Thomas, and A.J. Lee. 2011. "Erratum to 'State-Scale Evaluation of Renewable Electricity Policy: The Role of Renewable Electricity Credits and Carbon Taxes' [Energy Policy 39 (2)(2010) 950–960]." *Energy Policy* 39, no. 4, p. 2216.

Lin, S. 2008. "China's Value-Added Tax Reform, Capital Accumulation, and Welfare Implications." *China Economic Review* 19, no. 2, pp. 197–214.

Lu, C., Q. Tong, and X. Liu. 2010. "The Impacts of Carbon Tax and Complementary Policies on Chinese economy." *Energy Policy* 38, no.11, pp. 7278–85.

M.Mithani, D., S. Hassan, and A.R. Chik. 1998. "Trends and Patterns of Federal Government Spending in Malaysia." *Analisis* 5, nos. 1–2, pp. 67–87.

Manjit, S.K., and S.S. Banga, eds. 2013. *Combating Climate Change: An Agricultural Perspective*. Boca Raton, FL: CRC Press.

Martinsen, D., J. Linssen, P. Markewitz, and S. Vogele. 2007. "CCS: A future CO2 Mitigation Option for Germany?—A Bottom-Up Approach." *Energy Policy* 35, no. 4, pp. 2110–20.

Nakata, T., and A. Lamont. 2000. "Analyses of the Impacts of Carbon Taxes on Energy Systems in Japan." *Energy Policy* 29, no. 2, pp. 159–66.

Nachmany, M., S. Fankhauser, J. Davidová, N. Kingsmill, T. Landesman, H. Roppongi, P. Schleifer, J. Setzer, A. Sharman, C.S. Singleton, J. Sundaresan, and T. Townshend. 2015. *The 2015 Global Climate Legislation Study A Review of Climate Change Legislation in 99 Countries Summary for Policy-Makers*. London: The Grantham Research Institute on Climate Change and the Environment, and the Global Legislators Organization, and the International Organization of Parliaments.

Oh, T.H., and S.C. Chua. 2010. "Energy Efficiency and Carbon Trading Potential in Malaysia." *Renewable and Sustainable Energy Reviews* 14, no. 14, pp. 2095–103.

Painter, J. 2013. *Climate Change in the Media: Reporting Risk and Uncertainty*. London: I.B. Tauris & Co. Ltd and the Reuters Institute for the Study of Journalism, University of Oxford.

Pezzey, J.V., and A. Perak. 1998. "Reflections on the Double Dividend Debate." *Environ* 14.

Scrimgeour, F., L. Oxley, and K. Fatai. 2005. "Reducing Carbon Emissions? The Relative Effectiveness of Different Types of Environmental Tax: The Case of New Zealand." *Environmental Modelling & Software* 20, no. 11, pp. 1439–48.

Shoup, S.C. 1990. "Choosing Among Types of VATs." In *Value Added Taxation in Developing Countries*, eds. M. Gillis, C. Shoup, and G. Sicat. Washington, DC: World Bank.

Shrestha, R.M., and C.O.P. Marpaung. 1999. "Supply-and Demand-Side Effects of Carbon Tax in the Indonesian Power Sector: An Integrated Resource Planning Analyses." *Energy Policy* 27, no. 4, pp. 185–94.

Siriwardena, K., P. Wijayatunga, W. Fernando, R. Shrestha, and R. Attalage. 2007. "Economy Wide Emission Impacts of Carbon and Energy Tax in Electricity Supply Industry: A Case Study on Sri Lanka." *Energy Conversion and Management* 48, no. 7, pp. 1975–82.

Sterner, T. 2007. "Fuel Taxes: An Important Instrument for climate Policy." *Energy Policy* 35, no. 6, pp. 3194–202.

Sumner, J., L. Bird, and H. Smith. 2009. *Carbon Taxes: A Reveiw of Experience and Policy Design Considerations.* Colorado: National Renewable Energy Laboratory.

Werner, A., R.C. Brian, and T.M. Scott. 2001. "Is Free Trade Good for the Environment." *American Economic Review* 91, no. 4, pp. 877–908.

Wissema, W., and R. Dellink. 2007. "AGE Analyses of the Impact of a Carbon Energy Tax on the Irish economy." *Ecological Economics* 61, no. 4, pp. 671–83.

World Bank. 2016. "Malaysia Overview." http:// worldbank.org/ en/country/ malaysia/overview

Xing, Y. 2000. *Do Lax Environmental Regulations Attract Foreign Investment California.* Santa Barbara, CA: University of California.

Yusuf, A.A., and B. Resosudarmo. 2007. "On the Distributional Effect of CARBON TAX in Developing Countries the Case of Indonesia." Papers No. EEN0706, Economics and Environment Network, the Australian National University, 70.

Zhang, Z.X. 1998. "Macroeconomic Effects of CO2 Emission Limits: A Computable General Equilibrium Analyses for China." *Journal of Policy Modeling* 20, no. 2, pp. 213–50.

Zhang, Z.X., and A. Baranzini. 2004. "What do We Know about Carbon Taxes? An Inquiry into their Impacts on Competitiveness and Distribution of Income." *Energy Policy* 32, no. 4, pp. 507–18.

Zhaongxiang, Z. 2000. "Can China Afford to Commit Itself an Emissions Cap? An economic and Political Analyses." *Energy Economics* 22, no. 6, pp. 587–614.

Zhixin, Z., and L. Ya. 2011. "The Impact of Carbon Tax on Economic Growth in China." *Energy Procedia* 5, pp. 1757–61.

Zulfakar, M. September 24, 2014. "Malaysia will Continue to Cut Carbon Emissions, Najib Tells UN Climate Summit." *The Star.* http:// thestar.com. my/News/Nation/ 2014/09/24/Najib-New-York-Climate-cha nge/

CHAPTER 6

Does Mitigation and Adaptation Technologies in Rice Production Affect Product Price? Evidence from Japan

Misa Aoki

Introduction

According to the Fifth Assessment Report of the Intergovernmental Panel on Climate Change (IPCC), recent global temperature trends are attributable to human activities and have had significant impacts on global yield trends of certain crops (IPCC 2014). As food production depends heavily on climatic conditions and will therefore be severely affected by climate change (CC), every nation is concerned as to how the damages and benefits caused to agriculture by CC will affect domestic and international policies, trading patterns, resource use, regional planning, and ultimately the welfare of its people (Fischer et al. 2005).

Although changes caused by CC, such as increases in temperature or heavier rainfall, could enhance productivity and production of crops in some parts of the world, unexpected changes in environmental conditions could seriously decrease agricultural productivity and varieties in other regions (IPCC 2007). IPCC (2001) expects that rate of productivity increases in middle to high latitudes will diminish, and that yields will decrease in the tropics and subtropics. Food and Agriculture Organization (FAO) (2007) also reports that CC will increase vulnerability and even destabilize farming viability. These unstable conditions in agricultural production will lead to increases in food prices and make it difficult to feed the world's growing population. To stabilize food production under CC, appropriate technologies that consider socio-economic systems need to be adopted. The impact of CC on the agricultural sector affects not only production, but also the socio-economic status of the population.

While agriculture is affected by CC, food production is also a significant contributor to CC. Greenhouse gas (GHG) emissions from agriculture consist of CO_2 gases, methane (CH_4), and nitrous oxide (N_2O), produced from biological activity linked to bacterial decomposition processes in cropland and grassland soils and in the digestive systems of livestock. FAO (2014) indicates that such emissions include processes linked to enteric fermentation, manure management, rice cultivation, synthetic fertilizers, manure left on pasture, manure applied to soils, cultivation of organic soils, crop residue decay, prescribed burning of savannahs, and field burning of crop residues. According to FAO (2014), for the period 2001–2010 the largest emission source was agriculture, out of the sectors of agriculture, forestry, and other land use, while in 2011 total annual emissions from agriculture were 5,335 metric ton CO_2 equivalent, the highest level in history. As regards contributors to CC, Hodge (1993) points out that using excess synthetic fertilizers, pesticides, or herbicides for efficient mass production and mass distribution of farm products can cause GHG emissions. IPCC (2007) also shows that GHG emissions from the agricultural sector account for 10 to 12 percent of total annual emissions of CO_2. In addition, Scialabba and Muller (2013) point out that if other sectors related to agriculture and food such as the production of agricultural inputs, food handling and processing, and conversion from forest to farm land are considered, the total share of emissions from agriculture and food production accounts for at least one third of total emissions. This means that the agricultural sector is required to mitigate CC by introducing new technologies.

In this way, under future climatic and socio-economic pressures, the agricultural sector will be faced with challenges in selecting both mitigation and adaptation strategies. Regarding mitigation strategies in agricultural production, Rosenzweig and Tubiello (2007) suggest two key approaches: sequestration of atmospheric carbon in agricultural soil and the reduction of GHG releases to the atmosphere from agricultural operations. Examples of the former approach are irrigation, fertilization, rotation planting, agroforestry, and so on. The latter methods of mitigation include reducing incentives for cultivation or livestock raising and reducing chemical inputs and energy use in production processes. Organic and environment-friendly farming are thought to be one approach toward mitigating GHG emissions by reducing chemical inputs and managing soils. Flessa (2002) indicates that overall emissions of non-CO_2 gases could be reduced by about 25 percent by shifting to less chemically intensive, more organic production systems. On the other hand, adaptation strategies will vary with agricultural systems, locations, and CC scenarios. Focusing on agronomic technology, the possible adaptation strategies are to change planting strategies, cultivar types, and land management systems. There are additional dimensions to adaptation related to social and cultural aspects that might either favor or hinder the adoption of new techniques by farmers (Smith, Klein, and Huq 2003).

Choosing effective adaptation and mitigation strategies will represent a key challenge for farmers over the coming decades. Crucial decisions will have to be taken on whether new technological developments are to be adopted in practice. Various factors need to be considered in the adoption of new technology, including accessibility, knowledge of risks, and the impact of socio-economic pressures (IPCC 2001). Importantly, farmers have to maintain their livelihoods even after adopting new technologies. This indicates that market evaluation of farm goods produced using mitigating and adaptive methods are necessary. Given the additional costs of adopting new technologies and policies—including risk assessment and market research on transaction costs and price premiums—the existence of business and public subsidies is a significant incentive for farmers to make innovations (Parror, Olesen, and Hogh-Jensen 2006; Howden et al. 2007; Acs et al. 2009). Price premium has been extensively discussed in terms of agricultural goods produced using mitigation methods, for example organic, environment-friendly, low-input, and biodiversity-based farm products. However, few studies have examined the evaluation of farm goods produced in ways adaptive to CC. As Rosenzweig and Tubiello (2007) insist that adaptation strategies will often take precedence over mitigation, correct price evaluations of adaptive approaches could be important for the diffusion of appropriate technology for CC.

This chapter aims to investigate whether adaptation and mitigation technologies are evaluated in product prices in the market, focusing on rice production in Japan. The reason for the choice of Japanese rice production is that particular technologies for adaptation and mitigation have already been introduced in this country and goods produced using such technology have also been distributed in its domestic market. Although there are various technologies for adaptation and mitigation practiced in the field, this study focuses on the *introduction of high-temperature tolerant varieties* as an adaptive method and *reducing chemical inputs* as a mitigation strategy.

Rice Production in Japan

Rice Production in Japan to Date

The declining number of farmers, especially rice farmers, has been a major cause of concern in Japan as it is leading to heavy reliance on imported food, burdening the national economy (Namiki 2007). Table 6.1 shows trends of rice yield, productivity of rice, rice cultivation area, number of rice farmhouses, total number of farmhouses, and sales prices of rice in Japan. As Namiki (2007) points out, the decreasing number of farmhouses directly reduces the total yield of rice production. In addition, the average age of rice farmers has been increasing, reaching more than 65 years in 2010. Declines in sales prices have made it difficult to make a living by cultivating rice, which makes it hard to attract younger people to engage in rice farming.

Although rice production is in a strained situation, it has been given priority in national agricultural policies in order to maintain or increase self-sufficiency in food and to ensure food security. Prabhakar, Aoki, and Mashimo (2013) analyzed the relation between national agricultural policy and trends in Japan's agricultural situation and revealed that national agricultural policy in Japan has not been effective in addressing CC; policies taking account of CC should therefore be developed and implemented. New technologies for mitigation and adaptation in rice production will need to promote high productivity and create the added value required to maintain these levels of production.

Table 6.1 Trends of figures related to rice production in Japan

	1980	1985	1990	1995	2000	2005	2010
Yield (1,000 t)	9,692	11,613	10,463	10,724	9,472	9,062	8,478
Unit crop (kg/ha)	41.2	50.1	50.9	50.9	53.7	53.2	52.2
Unit crop (t/farmhouse)	544.0	686.4	766.6	779.5	809.7	997.1	1,104.9
Rice cultivation area (1,000 ha)	3,055	2,952	2,846	2,745	2,641	2,556	2,496
Number of rice farmhouses	1,781,552	1,691,990	1,364,862	1,375,774	1,169,762	908,819	767,300
Total number of farmhouses	2,604,119	2,131,181	1,964,997	1,902,690	1,668,478	1,346,217	1,153,298
Sales price (yen/60 kg)	18,495	19,384	18,010	17,473	14,291	13,289	11,369

Source: Created by the author based on Agricultural Census of each year from Ministry of Agriculture, Fishery and Forestry, Japan.

Impact of CC on Rice Production

According to researchers at the International Rice Research Institute (IRRI) it has been estimated that for each 1°C rise in average temperature, rice yields drop by about 10 percent. The International Food Policy Research Institute (2009) reported that yield losses in rice could be between 10 and 15 percent and that by 2050 rice prices will increase by between 32 and 37 percent as a result of CC. Nature Publishing Group (2008) notes that higher temperatures and increasing levels of carbon dioxide seem to lead to higher crop yields, but this is more than counterbalanced by other factors such as reduced water availability, worse problems with pests, difficulties in the timing of growing seasons, and, in particular, the impact of heat on flowering.

These phenomena may influence the production of Japan's main food crop, rice. Hayashi (2001) has found that rice production in central, western, and south-western Japan will be under increasing pressure from lower crop yields, while global warming may be advantageous for farmers in northern Japan. Specifically, if atmospheric temperatures increase by 3°C by the 2060s, potential crop yields will increase by 13 percent in Hokkaido, while decreasing by 8 to 15 percent south of Tohoku region.

Another change has been reported by Watanabe (2012), noting that CC leads to degradation in rice quality as well as changes in yield. This was shown by the fact that the ratio of first-class quality rice, which is usually around 80 percent, declined to 62 percent in 2010 when Japan experienced higher temperatures in summer. The ratio of first-class grain usually tends to be higher in northern areas than in southern areas in Japan, meaning that warmer temperatures will cause this ratio to decline more in the southern areas. MAFF (2014) demonstrated four main ways in which CC damages rice quality: white immature grains, immature grains, body division grains, and paddy rice spotted by stinkbugs. All of these problems occur under conditions of relatively high temperatures from July to September.

In order to maintain both productivity and the quality of rice, Hayashi (2001) suggests that farmers in central and southern Japan should begin to transplant crops later than usual to ensure that their plants do not flower at the hottest time of year, thus minimizing the risk of damage. They can also start planting new varieties that are resistant to high temperatures.

Mitigation Strategies in Rice Production

In Japan, mitigation strategies in crop production were introduced in 1999 when a basic national law, the "Food, Agriculture and Rural Areas Basic Act," was enacted. In particular, the Japanese government has promoted environment-friendly agricultural and organic farming methods that use less chemical fertilizers and pesticides than normal methods, along with the introduction of integrated pest management.[1]

In order to expand such environment-friendly farming, two types of certification system were established. One certifies farmers as "eco-farmers" while the other certifies crops produced in environment-friendly ways. The latter certification system is divided into two types: third sector certification systems such as organic JAS[2] and specially produced crops certified by local government. Standards of organic JAS are based on those of the International Federation of Organic Agriculture Movements (MAFF 2006), while criteria for specially produced crops differ from region to region.

According to census data for 2010, the proportion of farmhouses that have introduced soil management and reduced the use of chemical pesticides or synthetic fertilizers accounts for 48 percent of the total number of farmhouses, an increase of 1.7 percent from 2005. On the other hand, farmland for organic rice production did not increase or decrease from 2010 to 2013 and the ratio of land for organic crops has been consistent at 0.2 percent. The number of eco-farmers decreased slightly after reaching a peak in 2012. This might be led by the declining number of

---

[1] According to FAO, the definition of Integrated Pest Management (IPM) is the careful consideration of all available pest control techniques; the subsequent integration of appropriate measures that discourage pest populations; keeping pesticides and other interventions to levels that are economically justified; and reducing or minimizing risks to human health and the environment. IPM emphasizes the growth of a healthy crop with the least possible disruption to agro-ecosystems and encourages natural pest control mechanisms.

[2] JAS is the acronym for "Japanese Agricultural Standard," a term currently used to represent the overall certification system. The JAS system was introduced in 1950 as the Agricultural and Forestry Standard Law and assumed its current status in 1970 with the addition of the quality labeling standards system (MAFF 2006).

farmhouses, and the implementation of a new subsidy policy with more stringent conditions than the previous subsidy. As for specially produced crops, with 41 out of 47 prefectures managing their own certification systems, trends in the number of certified crops differ in each region.

Besides these strategies, the national government has also promoted biodiversity conservation in crop production and the introduction of energy-saving machines. Well-known practical examples of the former include biodiversity-friendly rice production in Shiga prefecture and "*konotori*-rice" cultivation, which helps to protect storks in paddy fields in Hyogo prefecture.

Mitigation technologies have, therefore, been introduced to some extent in rice production in Japan. However, for the further promotion of such technology, it is important to provide knowledge and economic incentives to producers in addition to research and development.

Adaptation Strategies in Rice Production

Introduced later than the implementation of mitigation strategies, adaptation strategy practices started in earnest from 2007. The main strategy is planting high-temperature tolerant new varieties, with many prefectural governments promoting other approaches such as later transplanting to avoid rice plants maturing during the highest seasonal temperatures and the control of water management. MAFF (2014) reported that these adaptive innovations are partly effective in reducing damage to immature grains.

As for introducing high-temperature tolerant new varieties, farmland for such new varieties has increased gradually in rice production. In 2010, it was 37,700 ha, which accounts for 0.23 percent of total paddy fields, but it increased to 65,300 ha or 0.41 percent of the total in 2013 (Table 6.2). This 1.7 times increase from 2010 to 2013 is considered to be a consequence of the unusually high temperatures Japan experienced in 2010. This warm season led to a drastic decrease in the proportion of first-class quality grain, from 80 to 62 percent.

In Japan, *koshihikari* is the most widely planted rice variety across the nation. This is because its grain is sold at the highest price with an evaluation of high quality and good taste. In this market situation, new rice varieties must not only feature high-temperature resistance, but also

Table 6.2 Newly introduced high-temperature tolerant varieties

Name of variety	Cultivation area (ha)				Increase from 2010 to 2013	Main prefecture(s)
	2010	2011	2012	2013		
Tsuyahime	2,537	3,648	8,560	9,831	3.9	Yamagata, Miyagi, Shimane, Nagasaki
Kinumusume	4,866	5,545	6,957	9,534	2.0	Osaka, Wakayama, Tottori, Shimane
Fusakogane	7,368	8,145	7,986	8,280	1.1	Chiba
Fusaotome	6,140	6,584	6,357	6,493	1.1	Chiba
Nikomaru	2,303	2,941	4,084	5,489	2.4	Shizuoka, Ehime, Kochi, Nagasaki, Oita
Sagabiyori	4,360	4,380	5,460	5,070	1.2	Saga
Genkidukusi	1,090	3,280	3,800	4,260	3.9	Fukuoka
Tentakaku	3,900	3,800	3,900	4,200	1.1	Toyama
Akisakari	347	1,100	1,690	2,600	7.5	Fukui
Yukinkomai	1,800	2,400	2,900	2,300	1.3	Nigata
Akihonami	852	1,634	2,140	2,175	2.6	Kagoshima
Tenkomori	930	1,200	1,300	1,400	1.5	Toyama
Others	1,234	1,374	1,552	3,643	3.0	
Total	37,700	46,000	55,800	65,300	1.7	

Source: Created by the author based on MAFF (2014).

good quality and taste. Table 6.2 indicates the names and cultivation areas of high-temperature tolerant new varieties and the main prefectures that have introduced these cultivars.

Of these cultivars, the growing area for *tsuyahime* accounts for 15 percent of total new variety cultivation. Certain prefectures throughout Japan started planting *tsuyahime* after 2010 because over 90 percent of its grain was evaluated as first class even though the average rate decreased to 62 percent in the unexpectedly hot summer of 2010. In addition, it has better taste and appearance than *koshihikari* and other varieties of rice (Asanome et al. 2009). Yamagata prefecture, which developed and first implemented this variety in 2008, promotes *tsuyahime* production and consumption, reinforcing the branding of this variety and diffusing it to other regions.

The variety that increased its cultivation area the most during 2010–2013 is *akisakari* in Fukui prefecture. In Fukui, the rice varieties used tend to concentrate on *koshihikari* under conditions where this variety is priced higher than others. This leads to many farmers planting and harvesting at the same time, resulting in late harvests and quality degradation. In addition, planting only one species makes production vulnerable to natural disasters caused by CC. Fukui prefecture researched and developed an original rice variety that has better taste and appearance than *koshihikari* (Tomita et al. 2009). In 2008, this new cultivar was registered as a promotional variety from Fukui prefecture and both government and local agricultural cooperatives started to plant it.

Other varieties have been developed for the purposes of reducing damage from CC and the branding of regional species. Some of these varieties are produced with mitigation technologies to reduce chemical inputs and conserve biodiversity.

Investigation of the Relationship between Product Prices and New Technologies

Product Prices and New Technologies

To investigate the relation between product prices and the introduction of new technologies for CC in rice production of Japan, the hedonic pricing method (HPM) is adopted. Ota (1980) explains that HPM is a way of identifying price factors according to the premise that price is determined both by internal characteristics of the good being sold and external factors affecting it. Models using this method usually derive the indicated prices by multiplying the related factors and logarithmically converting both members of this equality for use in regression analysis. The term HPM is attributed to Court (1939), who evaluated the price of automobiles. It is used to estimate the economic value of ecosystem or environmental services that directly affect market prices. The method is most often applied to estimate land prices that are influenced by environmental conditions.

In terms of fresh food, Waugh (1928) analyzed the prices of fresh vegetables by regressing these prices against various physical characteristics of the vegetables. In Japan, Kajikawa (1997) analyzed the price of apples, Hirooka and Matsumoto (1998) studied the example of beef, and Kurihara and Tanaka (2004) applied HPM to the price of green tea.

An earlier study on the price of rice was conducted by Kiminami, Kiminami, and Furusawa (2009). They analyzed the effect of branding rice on prices by using ordinary least squares regression (OLS), based on previous research which showed that the price of rice is affected by supply and demand, taste, quality, and branding (Terauchi 1998). In the more recent study, prices of 10 branded rice varieties including *koshi-hikari* were regressed by quality, yield, taste, and branding. To investigate the effect of branding on the rice price, dummy variables were introduced to indicate variety and popular brand. The results show that the price of branded rice is strongly influenced by taste, supply, quality, and brand. However, the study did not investigate the price premium for organic JAS or specially produced crops that use mitigation technology. According to data from MAFF, sales prices of these environment-friendly fresh crops are 1.05 to 1.42 times higher than crops produced in the usual ways. Given this context, it is necessary to include a variable indicating environment-friendly farming when determining rice prices. In addition, this study considers the effect of adaptation technology on price making by adding indicators for high-temperature resistant varieties to the model Kiminami, Kiminami, and Furusawa (2009) used previously.

Data

In order to estimate the effect of adaptation and mitigation technology on product price by HPM, data on the variables in Table 6.3 were collected. As price is affected by annual conditions, data for two years, 2013 and 2014, were used for this analysis.

The data indicating rice price, which is the dependent variable in the estimation model, show how much revenue in yen was transacted by both wholesale distributors and sales organizations such as collectives or cooperatives. It was obtained from *beikoku no torihiki ni kansuru houkoku* meaning a report of crop production provided by the MAFF. The amount of each rice variety produced was collected from the same source. The data show the number of tons marketed by both wholesalers and sales organizations at the time of pricing. The quality of rice is described by the variable *lnfirst*, the logarithmically converted ratio of first-class grains of each variety. The ratio was derived from MAFF's *kome no kensa kekka*, which reports the quality inspection results of different rice varieties every year. Evaluation of the taste of rice is based on data from Kokumotsuken-tei Kyoukai. This organization examines the taste qualities of major rice varieties. The results are reported in five categories: special A, A, A', B, and B'. The rice ranked in special A has the best combination of taste, while B' has the worst. For analysis, the ranks were expressed in numerically as indicated in Table 6.3. All the above figures were converted to logarithmic values in order to conduct the linear regression.

To indicate other features specific to a rice variety, *koshi, brand,* and *2013d* variables are included. *Koshi* shows whether the variety is *koshihikari* or not. It is necessary to consider this variety because, as Kiminami, Kiminami, and Furusawa (2009) pointed out, *koshihikari* is evaluated at higher prices than other varieties of rice. The variable *brand* also plays an important role in price making. Generally, a particular variety of rice produced in a specific place has a better evaluation in the market and is priced higher than others. To control for this tendency in the model, 10 varieties of rice produced in specific places which Kiminami, Kiminami, and Furusawa (2009) analyzed are added to the sample. The variable *2013d* indicates the difference between 2013 and 2014, since agricultural prices are influenced by the environmental conditions of each year.

Three other variables indicate whether a given variety of rice was produced using adaptation or mitigation technology for CC. The variable *lneco* indicates the proportion of eco-farmers using a given variety of rice out of the total number of rice farmhouses within a prefecture.

Figures in Table 6.3 show the number of rice farmhouses divided by total number of farmhouses multiplied by the number of eco-farmers in the same prefecture. The *Mitigation* variable indicates that the variety is produced using mitigation technology. In Japan, as the introduction of production technology depends on the decision of individual farmers, most varieties of rice are produced both in environment-friendly and in normal ways. However, some regions try to encourage mitigation technologies for a specific variety of rice for the purpose of gaining a price premium and creating a brand. Finally, the *adaptation* variable indicates whether the variety is high-temperature resistant.

Table 6.3 Variable explanation and descriptive statistics

Variable	Description	Mean	Std. Dev.
lnprice	Logarithmically converted rice price. The price was determined from sales organizations and wholesalers. Data source is *beikoku no torihiki ni kansuru houkoku* provided by MAFF in 2013 and 2014.	9.497	0.133
lnamo	Logarithmically converted amount of rice. The amount was determined from sales organizations and wholesalers at the time of pricing. Data source is *beikoku no torihiki ni kansuru houkoku* provided by MAFF for 2013 and 2014.	7.680	1.578
lnfirst	Logarithmically converted ratio of first-class grains of a given variety in 2013 and 2014. Data were obtained from *kome no kensa kekka* provided by MAFF.	4.356	0.410
lntaste	Logarithmically converted rank of rice taste. The rank was reported by Kokumotsukentei Kyoukai in 2013 and 2014. Ranks are indicated in 5 = special A, 4 = A, 3 = A', 2 = B, 1 = B'.	1.446	0.172
koshi	If the variety is *koshihikari* = 1, otherwise = 0.	0.304	0.465
brand	If the variety is a brand shown by Kiminami, Kiminami, and Furusawa (2009) = 1, otherwise = 2.	0.391	0.493
2013d	Data for 2013 = 1, otherwise = 0.	0.500	0.506
lneco	Logarithmically converted ratio of eco-farmers in the prefecture where the variety of rice is produced.	7.938	0.764
mitigation	If the variety is grown with mitigation technology = 1, otherwise = 0.	0.043	0.206
adaptation	If the variety is high-temperature resistant = 1, otherwise = 0.	0.304	0.465

Samples

The number of samples for the analysis is 46, which includes data from two years on 23 varieties and production regions. The samples are randomly chosen from monthly report on transactions of rice from MAFF. Seven of these are high-temperature tolerant varieties, while 10 are the highly branded varieties and production areas described in Kiminami, Kiminami, and Furusawa (2009) and the rest are nonhigh-temperature resistant varieties produced in the same prefecture as the adaptive varieties. This third type of rice is added to the analysis to accommodate the fact that pricing is generally specific to each region.

As high-temperature tolerant varieties, *tsuyahime* in Yamagata, *fusakogane* and *fusaotome* in Chiba, *tentakaku* in Toyama, *kinumusume* in Shimane, *sagabiyori* in Saga, and *nikomaru* in Nagasaki were selected as samples. As normal varieties for comparison, *koshihikari, haenuki, hitome-bore, yumeshizuku, hinohikari, kirara397, sasanishiki,* and *akitakomachi* were used in the regression analysis. Production locations include the prefectures above and Hokkaido, Iwate, Miyagi, Akita, Ibaragi, Niigata, and Nagano, which are all popular places for branded rice production in Japan.

Results and Discussion

Results of Regression Analysis

In the hedonic price equation, the dependent variable is the logarithm of the price of each variety of rice, while the independent variables are the other variables shown in Table 6.3. For analysis, OLS was adopted by using Stata12.1 based on Kiminami, Kiminami, and Furusawa (2009). Though the data can be treated and analyzed as time series data or panel data, OLS was chosen due to the limited number of samples. Taking heteroskedasticity into account, robust standard errors were used for estimation. This is because in the presence of heteroskedasticity neither t statistics nor F statistics are reliable (Wooldridge 2008). Three linear models were examined. Model 1 includes the variables of supply, quality, taste, year, and brand, excluding mitigation or adaptation technology. In Model 2, dummy variables of mitigation and adaption are added to

Model 1. Model 3 is the full model, which includes all the variables in Table 6.3. The ratio of eco-farmers is not a direct feature of rice variety because it shows the same figure for each variety in a given prefecture. Therefore, Model 2 which excludes this variable was examined separately.

The result of the regression is indicated in Table 6.4. The *R*-squared values of the three models are 0.599, 0.794, and 0.820, respectively, indicating that the overall fit of the hedonic price equation is relatively good. In addition, vif value of each model is less than 5, which means multicollinearity was not observed for all models.

The signs of the coefficients of each variable are consistent across all three models. Looking at *lnamo* indicating supply of the rice variety, all models show a negative sign which is statistically significant at the 5 percent level in the first and second models and at the 1 percent level in the third model. This means that larger amounts tend to reduce a variety's sales price, representing the normal relation between demand and supply in the market. From this result, the price determination of targeted rice varieties is based on the conventional theory of demand and supply.

To determine the effects of quality on prices, the variables *lnfirst* and *lntaste* are examined. Although the signs corresponding to *lnfirst* are negative in all models, statistical significance is observed only in the first two models at the 5 percent confidence level. The third model does not achieve statistical significance for this variable. These results show that higher percentages of first-class grain do not necessarily entail higher prices of a given variety of rice. Focusing next on the taste variable, these correlations are statistically significant at the 5 percent level in all models and their coefficients are positive and relatively large. As this shows that higher ranked rice varieties tend to be given higher prices in the market, the taste rankings provided by Kokumotsukentei Kyoukai are crucial for rice producers.

We next look at *koshi* and brand variables, which are also important for price making as mentioned in previous studies. The signs of *koshi* are positive in all models and statistically significant at the 5 percent level in Model 1 and at 1 percent levels in Models 2 and 3. This indicates that *koshihikari* varieties of rice can be transacted at a higher price than other varieties, attracting producers to plant this cultivar all over Japan. Given this, any new variety of rice must have quality levels equal to or higher

Table 6.4 Result of OLS regression analysis

	Model 1			Model 2			Model 3		
	Coefficient	t		Coefficient	t		Coefficient	t	
lnamo	−0.028	−2.48	**	−0.035	−2.52	**	−0.036	−2.88	***
	(0.011)			(0.014)			(0.013)		
lnfirst	−0.053	−2.26	**	−0.058	−2.51	**	−0.031	−1.00	
	(0.023)			(0.023)			(0.031)		
lntaste	0.266	2.36	**	0.201	2.42	**	0.188	2.42	**
	(0.113)			(0.083)			(0.078)		
koshi	0.060	2.47	**	0.069	2.88	***	0.074	3.10	***
	(0.024)			(0.024)			(0.024)		
brand	0.058	1.81	*	0.075	2.77	***	0.060	2.53	**
	(0.032)			(0.027)			(0.024)		
2013d	0.177	6.67	***	0.176	9.02	***	0.167	8.37	***
	(0.027)			(0.020)			(0.020)		
adaptaiom				−0.044	−1.2		−0.040	−1.19	
				(0.037)			(0.034)		
mitigation				0.313	5.51	***	0.288	5.18	***

	(1)	(2)	(3)
lneco			0.033
	(0.056)	(0.057)	(0.013)
			2.44 **
constant	9.430	9.587	9.248
	(0.136)	(0.099)	(0.177)
	69.2 ***	96.85 ***	52.39 ***
Samples	46	46	46
F statistics	12.63	21.65	23.18
R-squared	0.599	0.794	0.820

Note: The figures in parentheses indicate robust standard errors, while *, **, and *** indicate statistical significance at 10, 5, and 1 percent levels, respectively.

than *koshihikari* if it is to attract better prices in the market. As for brands that associate popular and well-known varieties with specific production locations, the signs of the coefficients are positive in all models, while significance levels differ among them. Since these significance levels are higher in Models 2 and 3, showing a better fit than the first model, brand seems to be an important factor in price making as well. This suggests that improving the level of consumers' or buyers' familiarity with a given rice variety and its specific production location could be significant for it being sold at higher prices.

The differences between the two years are shown by the dummy variable *2013d*. These coefficients are positive and statistically significant at the 1 percent level in all the models examined and their values are relatively large in comparison with the others. This shows that the conditions of a given year are likely to affect the price making of rice. In this analysis, prices in 2013 were higher than those in 2014.

The most important part of this analysis is the coefficients of *adaptation, mitigation,* and *lneco* which indicate the effects of introducing adaptation or mitigation technologies for CC on price making. As for the *adaptation* variable, it is statistically significant neither in Model 2 nor in Model 3. This implies that neither the implementation of adaptation technologies nor the introduction of new high-temperature resistant varieties is evaluated in product pricing in transactions. The signs of this coefficient are negative in both models, although they are not statistically significant. On the other hand, variables on mitigation technology show coefficients significant at the 1 percent confidence level for the *mitigation* variable and at 5 percent for the *lneco* variable. In these cases, the signs of all coefficients are positive. This result is consistent with the fact that sales prices of these environment-friendly fresh crops are 1.05–1.42 times higher than that of crops produced in the usual ways. This may be linked to early implementation of mitigation technology policies such as certification systems for farmers and farm products associated with environment-friendly practices. Furthermore, this feature has the advantage of attracting consumers who are concerned over food safety issues related to the use of chemical pesticides or synthetic fertilizers, leading more consumers to become familiar with these farming practices.

What Needs To Be Strengthened?

According to the regression analysis, supply, quality, brand, and harvest year can affect the product price of rice, the same result reported by Kiminami, Kiminami, and Furusawa (2009). The new findings of this study are that adaptation technology for CC in rice production is not evaluated in the product price, while mitigation technology is highly considered in pricing. The reasons for these tendencies need to be discussed here, because pricing plays an important role in diffusing new adaptive methods in rice production in Japan.

First, consumers and buyers have not been as well informed about adaptation methods in agricultural production to the extent that they have been about mitigation practices. This might be because the implementation of adaptation policies started much later than mitigation strategies in Japan. In addition, farm goods produced with mitigation technology can be made directly attractive to consumers in terms of food safety, as opposed to the more general issue of environmental conservation, as Nishiyama (2014) pointed out. Furthermore, in the research sector, there have been many studies on consumers' willingness to pay for organic food or environment-friendly farm products; most of these studies concluded that the willingness to pay for products associated with mitigation technology is higher than for products cultivated without this technology (Shimakawa, Sugiyama, and Tsuta 2008; Nishimura, Matsushita, and Fujie 2012). However, there have been few studies on consumer evaluation of products associated with adaptation technology.

Second, farmers and farmers' cooperatives engaged in production with adaptation technology do not give as much information on such technologies as they do for methods ensuring food safety. On the packaging or websites of these new varieties of rice, as investigated by the author, little information is given of high-temperature resistant varieties and their importance in adapting to CC. To obtain information on whether a rice variety is high-temperature tolerant, it is necessary to access the websites of prefectural agricultural experimental stations, while information on mitigation technology can easily be found on the websites or packaging of the relevant products. Even though consumers may have concerns with

CC and are willing to purchase adaptive products as a priority, to select the correct product is almost impossible due to the lack of information and the wide range of rice varieties displayed in retail or online shops.

Although the new varieties of rice produced with adaptation technologies face difficulties in obtaining high evaluations in the market, high-temperature resistant *tsuyahime* rice produced in Yamagata prefecture is priced as highly as the *koshihikari* variety produced in Nigata prefecture, which is well known for its good paddy fields. The possible reason for this tendency is that *tsuyahime* maintained its high quality even during the unexpectedly hot summer Japan experienced in 2010, while its taste was evaluated as better than *koshihikari* rice in each year. In addition to these features, *tsuyahime* rice is produced with less chemical pesticide and fertilizer and meets the standards for specially produced crops in Yamagata prefecture. Thus, *tsuyahime* rice production in Yamagata prefecture features both adaptation and mitigation technology. These results indicate that a good adaptive variety of rice combined with mitigation technology has the potential to be evaluated highly in the rice market in Japan.

Through a regression analysis, the relationship between price and technology implementation for adapting to or mitigating CC was revealed in this study. However, this study includes data for only 2 years and for 7 out of more than 13 varieties of high-temperature resistant rice, because the production and sale of new high-temperature tolerant varieties has only recently started in Japan. In order to investigate the relationship more deeply, data over longer periods and of more varieties of rice should be analyzed in future studies.

Conclusion

As CC may create unexpectedly serious conditions, the agricultural sector will be faced with challenges with regard to the introduction of both mitigation and adaptation strategies. This sector plays an important role not only in providing food security, which is a necessity of our existence, but also in maintaining socio-economic conditions by stabilizing the prices of crops. In particular, countries like Japan which have low self-sufficiency in food and depend greatly on imports are facing challenges in developing new varieties of plants that can produce consistent yields under a changeable climate and then diffusing these technologies in practice. In order to extend the technology, market evaluations are required of new types of crops produced with mitigation or adaptation technology.

This chapter aimed to reveal the effects of adaptation and mitigation technology in rice production on product price in the Japanese market. The Japanese government started to promote mitigation technology in the 1990s and adaptation strategies after 2000. Although a variety of technologies for adaptation and mitigation have been already been introduced and goods produced using such technology have been distributed in the domestic market, this study focuses on the introduction of high-temperature tolerant varieties as an adaptive method and on the reduction of chemical inputs as a mitigation strategy. By using publicly available data on price, amount, quality, and new technologies related to rice in Japan, regression analysis was conducted based on the hedonic price method.

The results show that supply, taste, brand, harvest year, and the introduction of mitigation technology can be seen to affect product prices, while adaptation technology, or the implementation of new high-temperature tolerant varieties, is not evaluated in product pricing.

The possible reasons for this lower evaluation of adaptation technology in the market are a lack of research and development of adaptive varieties of rice, less information being available to buyers or consumers, and little passive advertisement of adaptation technologies. These results imply that in order to diffuse newly developed varieties of rice which are adaptive to CC, these varieties must first have consistently high yields, good quality, and taste comparable or superior to *koshihikari* rice. After the establishment of new varieties and production processes, providing relevant information on these adaption technologies to consumers is essential, because these new technologies are not directly related to consumers' interests in purchasing products, as opposed to the case of environment-friendly farm products which can meet customer concerns over food safety. The introduction of adaptation technology commenced much later than the implementation of mitigation technology in Japan, resulting in consumers having more experience of mitigation technologies such as organic, low-input, and biodiversity-friendly farming. In this regard, not only producers, but also national and local governments and local agricultural cooperatives must strive to improve consumer recognition of these issues. In addition, the current study reveals that a combination of both mitigation and adaptation technology has the potential to be evaluated at higher product prices in the market, taking as an example *tsuyahime* variety production in Yamagata prefecture. Their approach, of producing high quality rice while ensuring food safety and mitigating CC in a specific region, possibly differentiates these products from others even of the same variety and enables the establishment of an original brand in the rice market.

Although not all new high-temperature tolerant varieties introduced in practice are considered in this analysis and only data accumulated over the short term are used, the study reveals important results regarding the relationships between rice price and mitigation or adaptation technology, allowing some policy suggestions. More detailed analysis will be necessary for further discussion after accumulating more data regarding new rice varieties.

References

Acs, S., P. Berentsen, R. Huirne, and M. Asseldonk. 2009. "Effect of Yield and Price Risk on Conversion from Conventional to Organic Farming." *The Australian Journal of Agricultural and Resource Economics* 53, no. 3, pp. 393–411.

Asanome, N., M. Moriya, K. Suzuki, and K. Ohtsubo. 2009. "Eating Quality Evaluation of New Rice Variety 'Tuyahime': II Comparison with 'Koshihikari' by Physicochemical Measurements." *Japanese Journal of Crop Science Extra Issue* 228, pp. 236–36.

Court, A.T. 1939. "Hedonic Price Indexes with Automotive Examples." In *The Dynamics of Automobile Demand*, 99–117. New York, NY: The General Motors Corporation.

FAO (Food and Agriculture Organization). 2007. *Adaptation to Climate Change in Agriculture Forestry and Fisheries: Perspective, Framework and Priorities.* Rome: FAO.

FAO (Food and Agriculture Organization). 2014. "Agriculture, Forestry and Other Land Use Emissions by Sources and Removals by Sinks." FAO Statistics Division Working Paper Series, Food and Agriculture Organization. Rome: FAO.

Fischer, G., M. Shah, F.N. Tubiello, and H. Velhuizen. 2005. "Socio-Economic and Climate Change Impacts on Agriculture: An Integrated Assessment, 1990–2080." *Philosophical Transactions of the Royal Society B* 360, no. 1463, pp. 2067–83.

Flessa, H., R. Ruser, P. Dörsch, T. Kamp, M.A. Jimenez, J.C. Munch, and F. Beese. 2002. "Integrated Evaluation of Greenhouse Gas Emissions (CO_2, CH_4, N_2O) from Two Farming Systems in Southern Germany." *Agriculture Ecosystems & Environment* 91, no. 1–3, pp. 175–89.

Hayashi, Y. 2001. "Ondanka ga Nihon no Suito Saibai ni Oyobosu Eikyo." *Agriculture and Horticulture* 76, no. 5, pp. 539–44.

Hirooka, H., and M. Matsumoto. 1998. "Wagakuni no Gyushiniku sijo Niokeru Kakakukettei ni Kanyo suru Youin." *Journal of Rural Economics* 69, no. 4, pp. 229–35.

Hodge, I. 1993. "Sustainability: Putting Principles into Practice. An application to agricultural systems." Paper presented to "Rural Economy and Society Study Group," Royal Holloway College, Egham, England.

Howden, S.M., J.F. Soussana, F.N. Tubiell, N. Chhetri, M. Dunlop, and H. Meinke. 2007. "Adapting Agriculture to Climate Change." *Proceedings of the National Academy of Sciences of the United States of America* 104, no. 50, pp. 19691–96.

IPCC (Intergovernmental Panel on Climate Change). 2001. *Climate Change 2001—IPCC Third Assessment Report.* Retrieved from http://ipcc.ch/ipccreports/tar/

IPCC (Intergovernmental Panel on Climate Change). 2007. "Synthesis Report." In *Fourth Assessment Report: Climate Change 2007*, eds. O.R.D. Metz, P/R. Bosch, R. Dave, and L.A. Meyer. Cambridge: Cambridge University Press.

IPCC (Intergovernmental Panel on Climate Change). 2014. *Climate Change 2014: Impacts, Adaptation, and Vulnerability.* Retrieved from http://ipcc-wg2.gov/AR5/report/full-report/

IFPRI (International Food Policy Research Institute). 2009. *Climate Change: Impact on Agriculture and Costs of Adaptation.* Washington, DC: International Food Policy Research Institute. Retrieved from http://ifpri.org/sites/default/files/publications/pr21.pdf

Kajikawa, C. 1997. "Ringo no Hinshitsu Tokusei to Kakaku Suizyun." *Journal of Rural Economics* 68, no. 4, pp. 199–206.

Kiminami, A., L. Kiminami, and S. Furusawa. 2009. "Analysis on Pricing Factors for Branded Rice in Japan." *Nihon Nogyo Keizai Gakkai Ronbunshu*, pp. 182–88.

Kurihara, Y., and H. Tanaka. 2004. "An Estimation of the Hedonic Price Function for Green Tea." *Japanese Journal of Farm Management* 42, no. 3, pp. 1–11.

MAFF (Ministry of Agriculture, Forestry and Fisheries). 2006. *Overview of the Revised JAS Law.* Chiyoda, Tokyo: MAFF. Retrieved from http://jasnet.or.jp/4-shuppanbutu/pamphlet/kaiseiJAS_e.pdf

MAFF (Ministry of Agriculture, Forestry and Fisheries). 2014. *Chikyu Ondanka Eikyo Chosa Repoto.* Chiyoda, Tokyo: MAFF. Retrieved from http://maff.go.jp/j/seisan/kankyo/ondanka/pdf/h25_ondanka_report.pdf.

Namiki, M. 2007. "Active Agricultural Population in Postwar Japan." *The Developing Economies* 7, no. 2, pp. 158–69.

Nature Publishing Group. 2008. *Climate Change: Impact on Japan.* Tokyo. Retrieved from http://natureasia.com/ja-jp/advertising/sponsors/climate-change/agriculture

Nishimura, T., K. Matsushita, and T. Fujie. 2012. "Consumer Willingness to Buy Biodiversity-Friendly Agricultural Products: The Role of Consumer Characteristics and Knowledge." *Journal of Food System Research* 18, no. 4, pp. 403–14.

Nishiyama, M. 2014. "Orutanatibu Nougyo to Fudosisutemu no Gendankai." In *Fudotyen to Chiikisaisei*, ed. O. Saito, 225–38. Tokyo: Nourintoukeikyoukai.

Ota, M. 1980. *Hinshitsu to Kakaku.* Tokyo: Sobunsya.

Parror, N., J.E. Olesen, and H. Hogh-Jensen. 2006. "Certified and Non-Certified Organic Farming in the Developing World." In *Global Development of Organic Agriculture: Challenges and Promises*, eds. N. Halberg, H.F. Alroe, M.T. Knusen, and E.S. Kristensen, 154–76. London: CABI Publishing.

Prabhakar, S.V.R.K., M. Aoki, and R. Mashimo. 2013. "How Adaptive Policies are in Japan and Can Adaptive Policies Mean Effective Policies? Some Implications for Governing Climate Change Adaptation." In *Governance Approaches for Mitigation and Adaptation to Climate Change in Asia*, eds. H. Ha and T.N. Dhakal, 103–18. London: Palgrave Macmillan Publishers.

Scialabba, N.E.H., and L.M. Muller. 2013. "Organic Agriculture and Climate Change." *Renewable Agriculture and Food Systems* 25, no. 2, pp. 158–69.

Shimakawa, Y., J. Sugiyama, and M. Tsuta. 2008. "The Impact of the Credibility Information on the Consumers' Buying Behaviour." *Report of National Food Research Institute* 72, pp. 107–11.

Smith, J.B., R.J.T. Klein, and S. Huq. 2003. *Climate Change, Adaptive Capacity, and Development.* London: Imperial College Press.

Terauchi, M. 1998. "Sanchi hinsyu meigara betsu uruchimai no hinsyu tokuseito kakakukeisei." *1998 Nenndo Nihon Nogyo Keizai Gakkai Ronbunsyu*, 152–57. Tokyo: Nosangyosonbunkakyokai.

Tomita, K., H. Hiroguchi, A. Kobayashi, M. Tanoi, I. Tanaka, T. Minobe, K. Kanda, T. Hayashi, K. Terada, A. Sigimoto, C. Kagoshima, and K. Higroguchi. 2009. "'Akisakari,' a New Rice Cultivar." *Fukui ken Nougyo Shikensyo Houkoku Syo* 46, pp. 1–21.

Watanabe, T. 2012. "What Level Does Climate Change Make Impacts on Agricultural Production, How to Address and How Should Agriculture, Forestry and Fishery Sector Tackle Climate Change?" Research project funded by MAFF. Retrieved from http://ccaff.dc.affrc.go.jp/conference2012/pdf/1-2_watanabe_abstract.pdf

Waugh, F.V. 1928. "Quality Factors Influencing Vegetable Prices." *Journal of Farm Economics* 10, no. 2, pp. 185–96.

Wooldridge, J.M. 2008. *Introductory Econometrics: A Modern Approach*, 4th ed. Toronto: South-Western Cengage Learning.

Further Reading

Food and Agriculture Organization of the United Nations. 2016. *Climate Change and Food Security: Risks and Responses*. Rome: Food and Agriculture Organization of the United Nations.

Kawasaki, J., and S. Herath. 2011. "Impact Assessment of Climate Change on Rice Production in Khon Kaen Province, Thailand." *Journal of International Society for Southeast Asian Agricultural Sciences* 17, no. 2, pp. 14–28.

Washio, K. 2013. "The Prediction of Climate Change and Rice Production in Japan." *Journal of Rice Research* 2, no. 1, p. e103. doi:10.4172/jrr.1000e103

CHAPTER 7

Climate Change Management: What Have We Learnt from the Asian Experience

Gamini Herath and Huong Ha

Introduction

Climate change is a global phenomenon that can profoundly alter Asia's economic future and livelihoods by exacerbating poverty and resource scarcity. One of the main causes of climate change is the increase in greenhouse gases (GHGs) emissions, primarily carbon dioxide (CO_2) (IPCC 2012, 2013; US Environmental Protection Agency 2016). Globalization since the 1980s and rapid industrialization in Asia, increased emission of GHGs raising temperatures and sea levels. Forest clearing in South East Asia destroyed considerable biodiversity and ecosystem services contributing to climate change. The Intergovernmental Panel on Climate Change (IPCC) (2007, 2014a, b) estimated that the temperature increase can range from 1.1°C to 6.4°C. Asia contributed 31 percent of global emissions in 2006 which is expected to rise to 42.1 percent of global emissions in 2030 (Shui and Robert 2006).

Asian developing countries have experienced climate change since the 1970s which has affected national economic growth. Economic liberalization created better incentives for rapid economic growth and poverty alleviation over the last three decades, but Asia's future growth can be affected by significant global warming and other climate change related problems (IPCC 2014a, b; Hulac 2016). Achieving poverty alleviation and addressing environmental-related issues will be a greater challenge in the context of climate change (Kellenberg and Mobarak 2011; Wedeman and Petruney 2016). The issues of sustainable development, poverty alleviation, and inequality in Asia have come under close scrutiny in recent years due to climate change which can disproportionately affect the poor and the vulnerable in developing countries in Asia. Thus, in this concluding chapter, we summarize the salient issues in the climate change debate in some Asian countries, mostly based on the seven chapters included in the book.

Impacts of Climate Change

According to the Asian Development Bank (2009, 2011), future growth of Asia would be led by seven countries: India, China, Indonesia, Japan, Korea, Malaysia, and Thailand which had a total population of 3.1 billion (78 percent of Asia) and a gross domestic product (GDP) of $14.2 trillion in 2010. By 2050, these seven economies alone could account for 45 percent of the global GDP (Asian Development Bank 2011). But this predicted growth trajectory can be vitiated by the unforeseen effects of climate change.

Climate change has already increased the intensity and frequency of precipitation, extreme rainfall, droughts, river and inland flooding, damaging crops such as rice, wheat, and maize (Lewis 2009; Iizumi and Ramankutty 2015). About 9 percent of the land in Malaysia is flood prone and the average damage due to floods has been estimated at RM100 million a year. The floods in the Malaysian state of Kelantan in 2014 displaced 200,000 people and the economic damage was estimated at RM1 billion (Davies 2015). This will affect food security, access to food, purchasing power, nutritional knowledge, and health affecting the livelihoods of millions of poor farmers in the region.

Increased variability of precipitation and increasing temperature may reduce water availability for crops including groundwater exacerbating water scarcity and food insecurity in rural areas (Chapter 2). In India, "the national per capita annual availability of water has reduced from 1,816 cubic meter in 2001 to 1,544 cubic meter in 2011. This is a reduction of 15 percent." (Suhag 2016, p. 2). Changes in glaciers have affected the Himalayas, ecosystem in the north-eastern region and the Indo-Gangetic plain resulting in water balance changes in river basins (Shrestha and Aryal 2011). According to Nandakumar et al. (2010), the amount of food required by India will be estimated at 253.3 metric tons by 2020. Yet, food may not be sufficient in the future. In India, climate change has increased severity of flooding specially in the Godavari and Mahanadi in the eastern coast. In Thailand, the 2011 flood affected 77 provinces, and reduced the world's industrial production by 2.5 percent (Haraguchi and Lall 2014). In December 2015, the government of the Philippines declared the state of "national calamity" after a series of floods and storms (AFP 2015, p. A19). Increase in rainfall can also increase the incidence of disease directly or indirectly, especially in northern Malaysia and coastal Sabah and Sarawak (Wu et al. 2016). The serious floods in the Perak, Pahang, Terenagan, and JKlanda in 2014–2015 in Malaysia are a case in point. A large number of people have been affected and dislocated by floods and cyclones in the Philippines (*FloodList* 2016).

Nepal is experiencing declining crop yields, pest and disease outbreaks, and invasive species (Budha 2015). This has affected food production which leads to food insecurity and increased losses of water, crop, and livestock (Chapter 2). Nepalese farmers are vulnerable and cannot adapt easily to climate change because of their poor socio-economic conditions. Climate change can increase hazards due to cultivation at hill slopes and other vulnerable areas where the poor are concentrated, pushing people into poverty and further exacerbating their reduced capacity to tide over disasters and adapt to climate change (Shepherd et al. 2013). The Asian Development Bank (2009, 2011) estimated that the Philippines, Indonesia, Vietnam, and Thailand would experience a reduction in the yield of rice of about 50 percent by 2100 compared to the level of rice yield in 1990. Wheat production can decline by 6 percent for each 1°C rise in temperature (*The Guardian* 2014). A drastic change is also inevitable in the forest ecosystem, which is expected to experience the decline of forest area and types (Stanturf et al. 2015). This change may result in the potential loss of forest biodiversity, but invasive species may thrive.

Adding into this, an increase in the population and climate change-related issues may lead to widespread starvation (Gahukar 2009). Natural disasters can widen the gap between the rich and the poor because many communities in rural Asia who depend on agriculture, forestry, and fisheries (Mutter 2010). Overall, climate change can affect fragile natural resource system and exacerbate economic and social inequalities both among the rural and urban poor.

Impacts on the Urban Areas

According to a report by the McKinsey Global Institute (Sankhe et al. 2010), the number of residents in Indian cities are expected to increase to more than one million by 2025. The urban population may reach 590 million by 2030 due to migration from rural areas (Singha et al. 2013). The city boundaries are generally planned for a specific amount of water, habitat, energy use, waste, transport, and green cover. Continued migration will upset this resource-planned balance and increase overexploitation of these resources leading to greater emissions severely affecting the urban residents (Singha et al. 2013).

The urban areas already suffer from serious environmental problems such as poor water supply, high energy cost, and waste disposal (Chapter 2). India and China have invested heavily on infrastructure, energy, water, and telecommunications for growth. There is a need to reexamine these development trajectories for mitigation of GHG emissions (Revi 2008; Ha and Dhakal 2013). The concept of compact cities that are conducive for healthy living and uses less fuel and energy consumption has emerged in urban planning in recent years. The focus should be on fuel management and energy efficiency, transportation economics and increased green space, and public transport and reduced pollution and proper waste disposal (European Union 2010).

Mitigation and Adaptation

Responding to climate change requires both adaptation and mitigation. Adaptation addresses near-term impacts and is an adjustment of communities to a changing climate. Mitigation is a longer-term process. Adaptation improves the capacity of the people to withstand against climate change impacts for some time. Planned adaptations are necessary which are multisectoral, and involves individual citizens and national governments.

National initiatives are important for climate change adaptation (Kim and Lim 2016). Multiple subregionally nuanced strategies may be required to respond to climate related crisis, such as food crisis, and cope with uncertainly (Food and Agriculture Organization of The United Nations 2016). The question of how to adapt still remains an important issue for many countries, including Malaysia, India, Bangladesh, and Nepal. Many farmers in India have adapted to water scarcity by changing the cropping patterns toward less water intensive crops (Khapre 2016). Changing cropping pattern is sustainable because they shift to less water using crops saving water. These adaptations by farmers may encourage others to adopt similar kinds of adaptations (Niles, Brown, and Dynes 2016). Adaptation should provide economic gains from the natural resources in exchange for the protection and conservation efforts extended by users. The economic gains should be sustainable, and the propositions aimed at economic gains should be socially accepted.

The Japanese government promoted mitigation technology in the 1990s and adaptation strategies after 2000 (Kuramochi 2014). The emphasis on environmental friendly agricultural and organic farming methods is notable in this regard (Chapter 6). New certification systems for "eco farms" are another innovation for mitigations of impact of climate change. The introduction of high-temperature tolerant rice varieties as an adaptive process might not be much favored by farmers (Chapter 6). Japanese farmers looked for additional salutary features such as high yields, good quality, and taste comparable or superior to Koshihikari rice (Wamboga-Mugirya 2016). The introduction of adaptation technology commenced much later than the implementation of mitigation technology in Japan, resulting in consumers having more experience of mitigation technologies such as organic, low-input, and biodiversity-friendly farming (Chapter 6).

Climate change mitigation is imperative to minimize emissions. Mitigation measures reduce emissions and enhance the sink function of the environment (carbon sequestration). Mitigation requires the identification of low carbon technologies with lower GHGs (Tanton 2013). It also needs considerable investment.

In addition, adaptation to natural disasters and climate change should also be taken into account in all development plans by better understanding of the interlinks between environment issues and disaster mitigation at various levels of action, and an appreciation of the need for multidisciplinarily understanding in disaster management as a whole (Hezri and Hasan 2006; IPCC 2007, 2012).

Legal Issues in Climate Change

Climate change will have significant impact on land, air, water, and oceans raising complex legal issues, especially in Asia where some countries do not have strong legal systems (Bradford 2005; *The Guardian* 2016). Robust legal frameworks that enshrine guidelines to mitigate the adverse impacts of climate change on the oceans, land, and air are imperative. Chapter 7 refers to specific situation in Malaysia and the response of the legal system to address climate change challenges. Malaysia's Ministry for the Environment is responsible for environmental laws. The Malaysian government appointed a National Climate Change Committee to formulate and implement effective strategies to mitigate impacts of climate change (Nachmany et al. 2016). But Malaysia's response to climate change were patchy and haphazard (Hezri and Hasan 2006). Future success of policies depends on how coherently these long-terms challenges are tackled (Raman 2009).

Some legal frameworks transcend national boundaries and are ratified by many nations and international bodies including the United Nations. The United Nations Convention on the Law of the Sea (UNCLOS) in 1982 established rules of governance in sharing oceans and their resources. It enshrines the notion that problems of ocean space are interrelated and complex (Global Ocean Commission 2014). The Convention signed in 1982 involves more than 150 countries addressing new legal concepts and regimes to provide a framework to develop specific areas of the law of the sea (United Nations 2012). Chapter 4 in the book specifically addresses this concern in South Asia. This is of great relevance because people living in Asian developing countries located in low altitudes are especially vulnerable to transboundary issues due to weak property rights and poor legal environment.

Complex legal issues may arise due to damage to coral reefs and fragile marine ecosystems. This will erode economic security of many countries in the Asia-Pacific region by removing vital fisheries habitats and under-mining the tourist industry (Willis et al. 2008; UNEP 2016). Marine spatial planning and designation of marine protected areas in coastal zones is important for states, regional fisheries management organiza-tions, and regional seas organizations requiring legal policy adjustments to their conservation and management regimes (UNEP World Conserva-tion Monitoring Centre 2008).

Sea-level rise can lead to the inundation of small islands (Maldives) raising jurisdictional issues over access to valuable marine resources and negotiation of maritime boundaries and resolution of disputes (Schofield and Freestone 2013). Also, "the majority of potential maritime bound-aries globally have yet to be settled and the Asia-Pacific region features multiple notable territorial and maritime disputes of long standing" (Prescott and Schofield 2005 cited in Warner and Schofield 2012, p. 10). Some countries in Asia have the view that UNCLOS is not effective because it does not address the issue of how to adapt and mitigate climate change (Chapter 4).

Awareness Education and Training

According to the UNEP (2006), all countries must promote the public awareness of climate change impact, and encourage both profit and not-for-profit organizations to respond to climate change. A low level of awareness of climate change impact is a hindrance to the success of climate change mitigation and adaptation. The public might change their attitudes and behavior if they were aware of the effect of climate change and were educated about climate change-related policies (the American Psychological Association Task Force on the Interface between Psychology and Global Climate Change, 2008–2009). What is most important is how awareness of sustainable development should be raised, how to change household's attitudes toward energy consumption, and builders' choice of construction technology and materials.

This needs incentives, education, well-designed policies and imple-mentation mechanisms, and other approaches. Managing human resources is a blockage in disaster management in China and Indonesia. Juban (2012) explained that strengthening human resources was an important task in the Philippines when dealing with the consequences of natural disasters, such as the spread of disease. The governments of a number of countries also acknowledged that institutional capacity for implementation of disaster management policy needed further improvement (Petz 2014).

Role of Gender and Diversity in Climate Change

Women play an important role in many Asian countries especially in agriculture, household demand for energy and water, and so on. Climate change can further burden women disproportionately compared to men due to socio-economic and cultural contexts (United Nations 2015a). The impacts depend not only on the biological differences but also the social roles. This is significant in Asia where women play a less dominant role in society (Hirschman 2016). In some countries there are many female-headed households. Many climate change policies are gender blind and this will not augur well for the future of women and sustainable development. Thus, governments must recognize that social stereotypes do not discriminate in climate change policy and against women's interests (UNDP 2013). The centrality of gender in adaptation strategies in agriculture and urban settings of farmers as a consequence of climate change has not been rigorously examined.

The Province of Davao del Norte in the Philippines is a good example of the need for inclusion of the residents' ideas, points of views, and perceptions toward socio-economic issues related to climate change since any policies and decision without consideration of their interest will place them in vulnerability to some extent (United Nations 2015b). Participation and democratizing decision making should be promoted by including those who are disadvantageous or marginalized based on income, occupation, ethnicity, race, and gender status. Thus, the authors suggested that social planning in any disaster risk management projects in the province should be gender sensitive, transparent, cost effective, and sustainable.

Overall, climate change impact has not been spared anybody or any groups of stakeholders. Often, women have faced higher risks and carried heavier burdens from the adverse effect of climate change due to many reasons, including lack of opportunities for employment and participation in decision-making processes, less capacity to respond to natural hazards (Alam, Bhatia, and Mawby 2015; Bossuet and Huyer 2016). Therefore, women's rights should be respected and women should be engaged more in the governance process of climate change (Bäthge 2010). It is important to improve "women's livelihoods and strengthen adaptation by ensuring women's access, control and ownership of resources," and ensure that relevant "education, training, awareness raising and information programs" are available to women (UNEP n.d., p. 6).

The Institutional Environment and Climate Change

Institutions are critical building blocks necessary for the development of a climate-resilient society. Institutions are the formal and informal organizations through which society structures share decision making and take collective action (McGray and Sokona 2012). The rules and norms through which people interact are also institutions. These institutions may need to evolve as the climate problem worsens (North 1990; Michonski and Levi 2010).

The challenge to climate resilience in developing Asia is that many institutions are weak or have become defunct. A strong institutional environment and good governance characterized by robust rules of the game is a prerequisite for success in mitigating climate change (Aicher 2014). Strong institutions lead to good governance principles and robust rules to effectively address climate change challenges (Davidson et al. 2006). Institutions dealing with use of natural resources play a major role in developing Asia. Collective action institutions are important, especially in Asia where weak property rights and corruption have hindered the full participation of all stakeholders in sharing the dividends of climate change-related policies. Governance refers to the authority, power, the dynamic interaction among the public sector, the private sector, the third sector (civil society), and academia (Ha and Dhakal 2013; Ha 2016). The degree to which these groups of stakeholders interact and intermingle determines how well the well-being of the public are protected. It is widely agreed that good governance is a vital principle to maintain social order (Wingqvist et al. 2012).

Governments with credible institutions can implement polices relevant to adaptation and mitigation. Countries with robust institutions suffer less death from natural disasters (Zoleta-Nantes 2002; Raschky 2008). For example the governmental institutions in Nepal are weak, and hence they cannot provide the recipients with adequate protection from climate change (Chapter 2). Strong political will and greater attention to these issues are imperative for successfully addressing issues of climate change. Poor governance has thwarted the effective implementation of climate change policies (United Nations 2008).

Climate change has not been confined within any country or any region, but its effect has transcended national boundaries, and thus new approach of global environmental governance is imperative (Ha 2013, 2014; Gillard et al. 2016). Some Asian countries do not have the capacity to unilaterally mitigate climate change. Regional and global initiatives require robust governmental institutions. Institutional capacity at the national and regional levels is necessary for relevant groups of stakeholders to negotiate bilateral or multilateral environmental agreements (Wingqvist et al. 2012). Mechanisms, instruments, formal and information arrangements, and institutions that go beyond state-led treaties have been explored. Given the complex and multidimensional nature of climate change, governments should further explore hybrid modes of governance, such as cogovernance, public-private partnerships, and social-private partnerships (Lemos and Agrawal 2006; Herath 2012; Ha and Dhakal 2013; Ha 2013, 2014, 2016). There were innumerable efforts in the recent past to gain the support of the local communities for the conservation of the Himalayan ecosystem, but they could not be sustained.

Resilience in the face of change is embedded in indigenous knowledge and know how (Chapter 3), diversified resources and livelihoods, social institutions and networks, and cultural values and attitudes. Policy responses to climate change should therefore support and enhance resilience (Adger et al. 2011). It is unfortunate, however, that many government policies limit options and reduce choices, thereby constraining, restricting, and undermining peoples' efforts to adapt. This is reflected in counterproductive policies, including those leading to increased sedentarization, restricted access to traditional territories, substitution of traditional livelihoods, impoverished crop or herd diversity, reduced harvesting opportunities, and erosion of the transmission of indigenous knowledge, values, attitudes, and worldviews.

Lessons Learnt–The Way Forward

Clearly robust strategies and policies are required to face the climate change challenge: adaptation and mitigation, population and social safety nets, natural resources conservation, legal and institutional frameworks, and national, regional and global environmental agreements (Hossain and Selvanathan 2011). The strategies must include direction (toward sustainability), distribution (inclusiveness), and diversity (multiple approaches, methods, and solutions). Uneven distribution of impacts and responses may reinforce existing inequality and vulnerability. Multidisciplinary dialogue and practices could ensure the emergence of effective synergetic responses to climate change.

Bottom-up processes can create the enabling conditions for all stakeholders to adapt to climate change, help build resilience among the rural and urban poor community (the most vulnerable to climate variability), and facilitate implementation of effective interventions to mitigate climate change.

Innovative policy interventions should promote adaptive capacity among vulnerable rural and urban communities (El-Ashry 2009). Mitigation reduces emissions and adaptation increases resilience of the natural environment. Mitigation and adaptation options are often context specific (Sommer et al. 2009). Each country is unique and will require a specific set of adaptation measures addressing the various scales of intervention and vulnerable groups.

Energy conservation, reduction of carbon dioxide and urban planning, reduction of illegal forest clearing, burning and logging, can help alleviate poverty among the vulnerable low-income populations. These should be the core elements to mitigate climate change in Malaysia, India, China, Indonesia, Bangladesh, and other Asian countries.

The emerging climate change crisis in Asia will cause serious resource problems and increased natural disasters. The technical and economic solutions to these problems are better known than the human and social issues. Newer participatory institutional frameworks should be explored to overcome the shortcomings of conventional approaches. The guiding thought must be close collaboration with local people, women, and indigenous populations to make adaptation and mitigation work. Thus, it is suggested that public services regarding infrastructure should be further improved, that is, taking into considerations Integrated River Basin Management, such as what Malaysia has done, to improve the current flood mitigation and adaptation systems.

Asia needs to identify new trajectories of research to address climate change. The interlinkages between mitigation and adaptation have not been well explored and further studies are warranted to better quantify the short- and long-term effects on suitability of mitigation and adaptation to climate change.

Research is needed into the processes and contents of national climate change frameworks (Prowse, Grist, and Sourang 2009). Information on adaptation methods implemented by the rural and urban poor, prioritization of sections of society, including women who are most vulnerable, and develop equitable adaptation and mitigation strategies should be an integral part of poverty alleviation. This will include innovations and understanding of formal and informal institutions, resource management, present levels of government support for adaptation and mitigation. Understanding and crafting appropriate adaptation and mitigation mechanisms require contextualized understanding of climate change. Judicious management of climate change requires understanding the environmental as well as economic, social, geographical, and political aspects. Attention to social aspects of climate change based upon empirically grounded understanding of the social reality is necessary.

Finally, international collaboration is essential to enter into global mitigation agreements but they need to be done through consensus. There is considerable work that remains to be done including refinements, extensions, new applications, innovative ideas, and more empirical assessments if climate change policy is to succeed.

References

Adger, W.N., K. Brown, D.R. Nelson, F. Berkes, H. Eakin, C. Folke, K. Galvin, L. Gunderson, M. Goulden, K. O'Brien, J. Ruitenbeek, and E.M. Tompkins. September/October 2011. *Resilience Implications of Policy Responses to Climate Change*, 757–766. Cambridge: Cambridge University press.

AFP (Agence France-Presse). December 20, 2015. "Philippines Declares State of 'National Calamity.'" *Straits Times World*, p. A19.

Aicher, C. 2014. "Discourse Practices in Environmental Governance: Social and Ecological Safeguards of REDD." *Biodiversity and Conservation* 23, no. 14, pp. 3543–60.

Alam, M., R. Bhatia, and B. Mawby. 2015. *Women and Climate Change: Impact and Agency in Human Rights, Security, and Economic Development*. Washington, DC: Georgetown Institute for Women, Peace and Security.

ADB (Asian Development Bank). 2009. *The Economics of Climate Change in Southeast Asia: A Regional Review*. Manila: Asian Development Bank.

ADB (Asian Development Bank). 2011. *ASIA 2050 Realizing the Asian Century*. Manila: Asian Development Bank.

Bossuet, J., and S. Huyer. 2016. *Gender and Climate Change Policy after COP21*. Frederiksberg: CCAFS Program, University of Copenhagen.

Bradford, J.F. 2005. "The Growing Prospects for Maritime Security Co-operation in Southeast Asia." *Naval War College Review* 58, no. 3, pp. 63–86.

Budha, P.B. 2015. "Current State of Knowledge on Invasive and Alien Fauna of Nepal." *Journal of Institute of Science and Technology* 20, no. 1, pp. 68–81.

Davidson, J., M. Lockwood, A. Curtis, E. Stratford, and R. Griffith. 2006. *Governance Principles for Regional Natural Resource Management*. Tasmania: University of Tasmania.

Davies, R. 2015. "Malaysia Floods—Kelantan Flooding Worst Recorded as Costs Rise to RM1 Billion." *FloodList*, Retrieved from http://floodlist.com/asia/malaysia-floods-kelantan-worst-recorded-costs

El-Ashry, M. 2009. *Adaptation to Climate Change: Building Resilience and Reducing Vulnerability*. New York, NY: United Nations.

European Union. 2010. *Making our Cities Attractive and Sustainable: How the EU Contributes to Improving the Urban Environment*. Luxembourg: European Union.

Food and Agriculture Organization of the United Nations. 2016. *Climate Change and Food Security: Risks and Responses*. Rome: Food and Agriculture Organization of the United Nations.

FloodList. 2016. "Death Toll Rises in Storm Hit Philippines: Government Declares 'State of National Calamity.'" *FloodList*, Retrieved from http://floodlist.com/asia/death-toll-rises-storm-philippines-december-2015

Gillard, R., A. Gouldson, J. Paavola, and J.V. Alstine. 2016. "Transformational Responses to Climate Change: Beyond a Systems Perspective of Social Change in Mitigation and Adaptation." *Wiley Interdisciplinary Reviews: Climate Change* 7, no. 2, pp. 251–65.

Global Ocean Commission. 2014. *From Decline to Recovery: A Rescue Package for the Global Ocean.* Oxford: Global Ocean Commission.

Ha, H. 2013. "Climate Change Governance: The Singapore Case." In *Governance Approaches to Mitigation and Adaptation of Climate Change in Asia*, eds. H. Ha and T.N. Dhakal, 182–99. London, UK: Palgrave Mcmillan.

Ha, H. 2014. "Land Use and Disaster Governance in Asia: An Introduction." In *Land and Disaster Management Strategies in Asia*, ed. H. Ha, 1–14. New Delhi: Springer.

Ha, H. 2016. *Governance Framework for Humanitarian and Disaster Response in ASEAN.* USA: Middle East Institute, Retrieved from http://mei.edu/content/map/governance-framework-human itarian-assistance-and-disaster-response-asean

Ha, H., and T.N. Dhakal. 2013. "Governance Approaches to Mitigation of and Adaptation to Climate Change in Asia: An Introduction." In *Governance Approaches to Mitigation of and Adaptation to Climate Change in Asia*, eds. H. Ha and T.N. Dhakal, 1–12. London, UK: Palgrave Mcmillan.

Haraguchi, M., and U. Lall. 2014. "Flood Risks and Impacts: A Case Study of Thailand's Floods in 2011 and Research Questions for Supply Chain Decision Making." *International Journal of Disaster Risk Reduction* 14, no. 3, pp. 256–72.

Herath, G. March 1, 2012. "Sustainable Agricultural Development in Malaysia with Special Reference to Food and Health Security and National Disasters." In *Impact of Increasing Flood Risk and Health Security in South East Asia, Proceedings of the International Symposium on Impacts of Increasing*, 85–92. Kyoto, Japan: Flood Risk on Food and Health Security in Southeast Asia.

Hezri, A.A., and M.N. Hasan. 2006. "Toward Sustainable Development: The Evaluation of Environmental Policy in Malaysia." *Natural Resources Forum* 30, no. 1, pp. 37–50.

Hirschman, C. 2016. "Gender, the Status of Women, and Family Structure in Malaysia." *Malaysian Journal of Economic Studies* 53, no. 1, pp. 33–50.

Hossain, M., and E. Selvanathan. 2011. "Population, Poverty and CO_2 Emissions in Asia." In *Climate Change and Growth in Asia*, eds. H. Hossain and E. Selvanathan, 17–51. Cheltenham, UK: Edward Elgar Publishing.

Hulac, B. 2016. "Top Economic Risk of 2016 Is Global Warming." *ClimateWire*, January 15.

IPCC (Intergovernmental Panel on Climate Change). 2007. *IPCC Fourth Assessment Report: Climate Change 2007.* Geneva, Switzerland: The IPCC Secretariat.

IPCC (Intergovernmental Panel on Climate Change). 2012. *Managing the Risks of Extreme Events and Disasters to Advance Climate Change Adaptation.* Cambridge: Cambridge University Press.

IPCC (Intergovernmental Panel on Climate Change). 2013. "Climate Change 2013: The Physical Science Basis." Working Group I contribution to the IPCC Fifth Assessment Report. Cambridge, UK: Cambridge University Press. Retrieved from www.ipcc.ch/report/ar5/wg1

IPCC (Intergovernmental Panel on Climate Change). 2014a. "Climate Change 2014: Synthesis Report." Contribution of Working Groups I, II and III to the Fifth Assessment Report of the Intergovernmental Panel on Climate Change [Core Writing Team, R.K. Pachauri and L.A. Meyer (eds.)]. Geneva, Switzerland: The IPCC Secretariat.

IPCC (Intergovernmental Panel on Climate Change). 2014b. "Summary for policymakers." In: *Climate Change 2014: Impacts, Adaptation, and Vulnerability. Part A: Global and Sectoral Aspects.* Contribution of Working Group II to the Fifth Assessment Report of the Intergovernmental Panel on Climate Change [Field, C.B., V.R. Barros, D.J. Dokken, K.J. Mach, M.D. Mastrandrea, T.E. Bilir, M. Chatterjee, K.L. Ebi, Y .O. Estrada, R.C. Genova, B. Girma, E.S. Kissel, A.N. Levy, S. MacCracken, P .R. Mastrandrea, and L.L. White (eds.)]. Cambridge University Press, Cambridge, United Kingdom and New York, NY, USA, pp. 1-32.

Iizumi, T., and N. Ramankutty. March 2015. "How do Weather and Climate Influence Cropping Area and Intensity?" *Global Food Security* 4, pp. 46–50. http://sciencedirect.com/science/article/pii/S22119124 14000583 - aff0010

Juban, N. March 1, 2012. "The Epidemiology of Disasters: Health Effects of Disasters in the Philippines." In *Impact of Increasing Flood Risk and Health Security in South East Asia*, Proceedings of the International Symposium on Impacts of Increasing Flood Risk on food and Health Security in Southeast Asia, 53–60. Kyoto, Japan: Flood Risk on Food and Health Security.

Kellenberg, D., and A.M. Mobarak. 2011. "The Economics of Natural Disasters." *Annual Review of Resource Economics* 3, no. 1, pp. 297–312.

Khapre, S. 2016. "Maharashtra: New Crop Pattern for Drought-Hit Districts." *The Indian Express*, April 16, Retrieved from http://indianexpress.com/article/india/india-news-india/maharashtra-water-crisis-crop-pattern-drought-2755744/

Kim, D., and U. Lim. 2016. "Urban Resilience in Climate Change Adaptation: A Conceptual Framework." *Sustainability* 8, no. 5, 405. doi:10.3390/su8040405

Kuramochi, T. 2014. *Ghg Mitigation in Japan: An Overview of the Current Policy Landscape.* Washington, DC: World Resources Institute.

Lemos, M.C., and A. Agrawal. 2008. "Environmental Governance." *Annual Review of Environmental Resources* 31, no. 1, pp. 297–325.

Lewis, J.I. 2009. "Climate Change and Security: Examining China's Challenges in a Warming World." *International Affairs* 85, no. 6, pp. 1195–213.

McGray, H., and Y. Sokona. 2012. *Why Institutions Matter for Climate Change Adaptation in Developing Countries*. Washington, DC: World Resources Institute.

Michonski, K., and M.A. Levi. 2010. *Harnessing International Institutions to Address Climate Change*. New York, NY: Council on Foreign Relations®, Inc.

Mutter, J. 2010. "Disasters Widen the Rich–Poor Gap'." *Nature* 466, no. 7310, 1042. doi:10.1038/4661042a

Nandakumar, T., K. Ganguly, P. Sharma, and A. Gulati. 2010. *Food and Nutrition Security Status in India Opportunities for Investment Partnerships*. Manila: Asian Development Bank.

Niles, M.T., M. Brown, and R. Dynes. 2016. "Farmer's Intended and Actual Adoption of Climate Change Mitigation and Adaptation Strategies." *Climatic Change* 135, no. 2, pp. 277–95.

North, D. 1990. *Institutions, Institutional Change and Economic Performance*. Cambridge: Cambridge University Press.

Petz, D. 2014. *Strengthening Regional and National Capacity for Disaster Risk Management: The Case of ASEAN*. Washington, DC: Brookings Institution.

Prowse, T., N. Grist, and C. Sourang. 2009. *Closing the Gap between Climate Adaptation and Poverty Reduction Frameworks*. London: Overseas Development Institute.

Raman, H.A. 2009. "Global Climate Change and its Effect on Human Habitat and Environment in Malaysia." *Malaysian Journal of Environmental Management* 10, pp. 17–32.

Raschky, P.A. 2008. "Institutions and the Losses from Natural Disasters." *Natural Hazards and Earth System Sciences* 8, no. 4, pp. 627–34.

Revi, A. 2008. "Climate Change Risk: An Adaptation and Mitigation Agenda for Indian Cities." *Environment and Urbanisation* 20, no. 1, pp. 207–29.

Sankhe, S., I. Vittal, R. Dobbs, A. Mohan, A. Gulati, J. Ablett, S. Gupta, A. Kim, S. Paul, A. Sanghvi, and G. Sethy. 2010. *India's Urban Awakening: Building Inclusive Cities, Sustaining Economic Growth*. India: The McKinsey Global Institute.

Schofield, C., and D. Freestone. 2013. "Options to Protect Coastlines and Secure Maritime Jurisdictional Claims in the Face of Global Sea Level Rise." In *Threatened Island Nations Legal Implications of Rising Seas and a Changing Climate*, eds. M.B. Gerrard and G.E. Wannier, 141–65. New South Wales: University of Wollongong.

Sommer, S.G., J.E. Olesen, S.O. Petersen, M.R. Weisbjerg, L. Valli, L. Rodhe, and F. e'Line. 2009. "Region-Specific Assessment of Greenhouse Gas Mitigation with Different Manure Management Strategies in Four Agroeco-Logical Zones." *Global Change Biology* 15, no. 12, pp. 2825–37.

Shepherd, A., T. Mitchell, K. Lewis, A. Lenhardt, L. Jones, L. Scott, and R. Muir-Wood. 2013. *The Geography of Poverty, Disasters and Climate Extremes in 2030.* London, UK: ODI.

Shrestha, A.B., and R. Aryal. 2011. "Climate Change in Nepal and its Impact on Himalayan Glaciers." *Regional Environmental Change* 11, no. 1, pp. 65–77.

Shui, B., and R.C. Robert. 2006. "The Role of CO_2 Embodiment in US-China Trade." *Energy Policy* 34, no. 18, pp. 4063–69.

Singha, A.K., S. Majumdar, A. Saha, and S. Hazra. 2013. "De-Constructing Debate on National Action Plan on Climate Change at the state level: A Case Study of Meghalaya State, India." In *Governance Approaches to Mitigation of and Adaptation to Climate Change in Asia*, eds. H. Ha and T.N. Dhakal. Basingstoke: Palgrave Macmillan.

Stanturf, J.A., P. Kant, J.P.B. Lillesø, S. Mansourian, M. Kleine, L. Graudal, and P. Madsen. 2015. *Forest Landscape Restoration as a Key Component of Climate Change Mitigation and Adaptation. IUFRO World Series Volume 34.* Vienna: International Union of Forest Research Organizations (IUFRO).

Sommer, S.G., J.E. Olesen, S.O. Petersen, M.R. Weisbjerg, L. Valli, L. Rodhe, and F. Be'Line. 2009. "Region-specific Assessment of Greenhouse Gas Mitigation with Different Manure Management Strategies in Four Agro-Ecological Zones." *Global Change Biology* 15, no. 12, pp. 2825–37.

Suhag, R. 2016. *Overview of Ground Water in India.* New Delhi: PRS Legislative Research.

The Guardian. 2014. "Global Warming Will Cut Wheat Yields, Research Shows." *The Guardian*, Retrieved December 23 from https://theguardian.com/environment/2014/ dec/23/global-warming-cut-wheat-yields-research-shows

The Guardian. July 27, 2016. "Climate Models are Accurately Predicting Ocean and Global Warming." Retrieved from https://theguardian.com/environment/climate-consensus-97-per-cent/2016/jul/27/climate-models-are-accurately-predicting-ocean-and-global-warming

The American Psychological Association Task Force on the Interface between Psychology and Global Climate Change. 2008–2009. *Psychology & Global Climate Change Addressing a Multifaceted Phenomenon and Set of Challenges.* Washington, DC: American Psychological Association.

UNDP (United Nations Development Programme). 2013. *Overview of Linkages Between Gender "Recent Studies Reveal that Not and Climate Change.* New York, NY: UNDP.

UNEP (United Nations Development Programme). n.d. *Women at the Frontline of Climate Change Gender Risks and Hopes.* Nairobi: UNEP.

UNEP (United Nations Development Programme). 2006. *Raising Awareness of Climate Change: A Handbook for Government Focal Points.* Geneva: UNEP.

UNEP and World Conservation Monitoring Centre. 2008. *National and Regional Networks of Marine Protected Areas: A Review of Progress.* Cambridge: UNEP and World Conservation Monitoring Centre.

United Nations. 2008. *Achieving Sustainable Development and Promoting Development Cooperation.* New York, NY: United Nations.

United Nations. 2012. *UNCLOS at 30.* New York, NY: United Nations.

United Nations. 2015a. *As Climate Change Affects More Women than Men, States Must "Step Up" Gender-Focused Efforts, Political Will, Delegates Tell Commission.* New York, NY: United Nations. Retrieved from http://un.org/press/en/2015/wom2029. doc.htm

United Nations. 2015b. *Policy Integration in Government in Pursuit of the Sustainable Development Goals.* New York, NY: United Nations.

United Nations Human Settlements Programme. n.d. *Urban Patterns for a Green Economy Optimising Infrastructure.* Nairobi: United Nations Human Settlements Programme.

US Environmental Protection Agency. 2016. *Climate Change Indicators: Greenhouse Gases.* Washington, DC: US Environmental Protection Agency.

Wamboga-Mugirya, P. 2016. "New Rice Seed Promises High Yields, Income." *Daily Monitor,* Retrieved from http://monitor.co.ug/Magazines/Farming/New-rice-seed-promises-high-yields--income/-/689860/3118674/-/e2dokn/-/index.html

Warner, R., and C. Schofield. 2012. "Climate Change and the Oceans: Legal and Policy Portents for the Asia Pacific Region and Beyond." In *Climate Change and the Oceans: Gauging the Legal and Policy Currents in the Asia Pacific and Beyond*, eds. R. Warner and C. Schofield, 1–20. New South Wales: University of Wollongong.

Wedeman, N., and T. Petruney. 2016. *Invest in Women to Tackle Climate Change and Conserve the Environment.* New York, NY: Women Deliver.

Wingqvist, G.Ö., O. Drakenberg, D. Slunge, M. Sjöstedt, and A. Ekbom. 2012. *The Role of Governance for Improved Environmental Outcomes.* Bromma: Swedish Environmental Protection Agency.

Wu, X., Y. Lu, S. Zhou, L. Chen, and B. Xu. 2016. "Impact of Climate Change on Human Infectious Diseases: Empirical Evidence and Human Adaptation." *Environment International* 86, pp. 14–23.

Zoleta-Nantes, D.B. 2002. "Differential Impacts of Flood Hazard Risk Among Street Children, the Urban Poor and Residents of Wealthy Neighbourhoods in Metro Manila, Philippines." *Mitigation and Adaptation Strategies for Global Change* 7, no. 3, pp. 239–66.

Further/Suggested Reading

Barnett, J., and W. Adger. 2007. "Climate Change, Human Security and Violent Conflict." *Political Geography* 26, no. 6, pp. 639–55.

Dobson, A. 2004. *Citizenship and the Environment.* New York, NY: Oxford University Press.

Dobson, A. 2014. *Listening for Democracy: Recognition, Representation, Reconciliation.* Oxford: *Oxford University Press.*

Ferrer, J., M.A. Perez-Martin, S. Jiminez, T. Estrela, and J. Andreu. 2012. "GIS-Based Models for Water Quantity and Quality Assessment in the Júcar River Basin, Spain, Including Climate Change Effects." *Science of the Total Environment* 440, pp. 42–59.

Ha, H., and T.N. Dhakal, eds. 2013. *Governance Approaches to Mitigation and Adaptation of Climate Change in Asia.* London, UK: Palgrave Mcmillan.

Kelly, P.M., and W.N. Adger. 2000. "Theory and Practice in Assessing Vulnerability to Climate Change and Facilitating Adaptation." *Climatic Change* 47, no. 4, pp. 325–52.

Nasrin, S., A. Baskaran, and R.Q.Q. Rasiah. 2016. "Microfinance and Savings Among the Poor: Evidence from Bangladesh Microfinance Sector." *Quality and Quantity* 51, no. 4, 1–14. doi:10.1007/s11135-016-0342-1

Newhall, C.G., and S. Self. 1982. "The Volcanic Explosivity Index (VEI): An Estimate of Explosive Magnitude for Historical Volcanism." *Journal Geophysical Research* 87, no. C2, pp. 1231–38.

Nisbet, E.K., and M.L. Gick. 2008. "Can Health Psychology Help the Planet? Applying Theory and Models of Health Behaviour to Environmental Actions." *Canadian Psychology/Psychologie canadienne* 49, no. 4, pp. 296–303.

Okpara, U.T., L.C. Stringer, and A.J. Dougill. 2016. "Perspectives on Contextual Vulnerability in Discourses of Climate Conflict." *Earth System Dynamics* 7, no. 1, pp. 89–102.

Parikh, J., and K. Parikh. 2011. "India's Energy Needs and Low Carbon Options." *Energy* 36, no. 6, 3650–58. doi:10.1016/j.energy.2011.01.046

Rai, Y.K., B.B. Ale, and J. Alam. 2012. "Impact Assessment of Climate Change on Paddy Yield: A Case Study of Nepal Agriculture Research Council (NARC), Tarahara, Nepal." *Journal of the Institute of Engineering* 8, no. 3, pp. 147–67.

Rekadwad, B.N., and C.N. Khobragade. December 2016. "Is the Increase in Oil Pollution a Possibility of the Presence of Diverse Microorganisms? An Experimental Dataset on Oil Prevalent Areas of Goa, India." *Data in Brief* 9, pp. 8–12.

Scialabba, N.E.H., and L.M. Muller. 2013. "Organic Agriculture and Climate Change." *Renewable Agriculture and Food Systems* 25, no. 2, pp. 158–69.

Sethi, M. 2014. "Location of Greenhouse Gases (GHG) Emissions from Thermal Power Plants in India Along the Urban-Rural Continuum." *Journal of Cleaner Production* 103, 586–600. doi:10.1016/j.jclepro.2014.10.067

Tashmin, N. 2016. "Can Climate Finance in Bangladesh be Helpful in Making Transformational Change in Ecosystem Management?" *Environmental Systems Research* 5, no. 1, 2. doi:10.1186/s40068-016-0054-5

United Nations. 2015. *Policy Integration in Government in Pursuit of the Sustainable Development Goals*. New York, NY: United Nations.

Yale Center for Environmental Law & Policy and Center for International Earth Science Information Network. 2016. *2016 Environmental Performance Index*. New Haven, CT and Palisades, NY: Yale Center for Environmental Law & Policy.

About the Author

Dr. Huong Ha is currently affiliated with School of Business, Singapore University of Social Sciences. She has been affiliated with UON Singapore and University of Newcastle, Australia. Her previous positions include Dean, Director of Research and Development, Deputy Course Director, Chief Editor, Executive Director, Business Development manager, and so on. She holds a PhD from Monash University (Australia) and a master's degree from National University of Singapore. She was a recipient of a PhD scholarship (Monash University), Temasek scholarship (National University of Singapore), and a scholarship awarded by the United Nations University/International Leadership Academy, and many other scholarships, professional and academic awards, and research-related grants.

She has authored or coedited the following books: (i) Ha, Huong (2014). *Change Management for Sustainability*. USA: Business Expert Press; (ii) Ha, Huong (Ed.) (2014). *Land and Disaster Management Strategies in Asia*. Springer; (iii) Ha, Huong, and Dhakal, T. N. (Eds.) (2013). *Governance Approaches to Mitigation of and Adaptation to Climate Change in Asia*. Basingstoke: Palgrave Macmillan; and (iv) Ha, Huong; Fernando, Lalitha, and Mahmood, Amir (2015), *Strategic Disaster Risk Management in Asia*, Springer. She has produced about 75 journal articles, book chapters, conference papers, and articles in encyclopedias. She has been an invited member of (i) the international editorial boards of many international journals and book projects; (ii) the scientific and technical committees of several international conferences in many countries; and (iii) international advisory board of many associations. She has also been a reviewer of many international journals and international conferences.

List of Contributors

Dr. Hui Shan Loh is currently a lecturer at Singapore University of Social Sciences (SUSS). She received a BSc (Maritime Studies), MSc (Logistics) and a PhD degree in Maritime Studies from NTU in 2008, 2010 and 2015, respectively. Before joining SUSS, Hui Shan worked as Research Fellow at NTU, and Assistant Manager at The Maritime and Port Authority of Singapore.

Dr. Bimal Raj Regmi is currently working as governance specialist in International Centre for Integrated Mountain Development (ICIMOD). He has more than 17 years of academic and professional experience in climate change and natural resource management. He has specific expertise on climate change adaptation governance issues specific to the understanding of agriculture and natural resource management. He has contributed as an author in a number of publications on climate change and natural resource management. Contact: bimalrocks@yahoo.com

Mr. Apar Paudyal is currently working as a climate change program officer in Practical Action South Asia. Apar has more than eight years of experiences in environment and climate change. He is particularly interested in policy and practices of climate change adaptation and the cutting edge issues related to climate governance, financing, and technology transfer. Contact: apar.paudyal@practicalaction.org.np

Dr. rer. nat. Claus-Peter Rückemann is a senior lecturer and researcher at the Leibniz Universität Hannover and the Westfälische Wilhelms-Universität Münster (WWU), Germany. He holds a university-diploma degree in geophysics and a doctorate degree for natural sciences in geoinformatics, informatics, and geosciences from the faculty of mathematical and natural sciences, WWU. Dr. Rückemann teaches information science, security, and computing at the University of Hannover. He studied geophysics, theoretical and applied physics, mathematics, computer science, and archaeology. He is the chair of the board on Advanced Computing and Emerging Technologies and the chair of the Symposia Board of the International Academy, Research, and Industry Association (IARIA), general chair of the International Conference on Advanced Communications and Computation (INFOCOMP), head of research of the LX Foundation, director of the GEXI Consortium. Dr. Rückemann serves as member and chair of more than 20 international boards and committees, spanning Northern America, Europe, Middle East, and Asia. Dr. Rückemann is the author of numerous scientific publications awarded with more than a dozen international best paper awards and has been distinguished with the Grade IARIA Fellow for his scientific research on the state of the art improvement in HPC, information systems, distributed computing, and international collaboration.

Dr Shivani Raswan Pathania received her doctorate of philosophy (PhD) (international law) from Guru Nanak Dev University, Amritsar, Punjab.

Dr. Olivia Tan Swee Leng was a legal counsel of Kuala Lumpur Regional Centre for Arbitration (KLRCA) and she was in-charge of the domain name dispute resolution, for both .com from Asian Domain Name Dispute Resolution Centre (ADNDRC), .my cases at KLRCA and mediation/arbitration case management. She obtained her bachelor of law degree with honors at University of London (UK) (1993), completed her CLP in the year 1996, master at law at the National University of Malaysia (UKM) in the year 2002 and PhD (law) at the National University of Malaysia (UKM) in the year 2014. She was the book prize winner for civil procedure paper and general paper awarded by the Certificate of Legal Practice Board (Malaysia) in the Year 1996. She practiced as an advocate and solicitor in Malaysia in the area of corporate litigation, intellectual property (trademark), banking and conveyancing. Currently, Dr. Olivia is a lecturer and deputy director for Collaboration and Innovation (CIC) at Multimedia University, Cyberjaya, Malaysia.

Dr. Misa Aoki is currently an assistant professor of Nara Women's University Faculty of Human Life and Environment, Nara, Japan. She works on the issues relevant to behavioral changes of small-household farmers due to national or local government policies in Japan and other Asian countries. Specifically, she identified causes for agriculture policies and sustainable agriculture policies from the viewpoint of micro economics. In addition, she studies consumers' behavior toward environmentally friendly farm crops at farmers' market in Japan. She obtained her master's degree from Kyoto University Graduate School of Global Environmental Studies in 2010 and PhD from Nara Women's University Graduate School of Humanities and Sciences in 2015.

Dr. Gamini Herath is professor of economics at the School of Business, Monash University Malaysia. He is also the director of the Social and Economic Transformation in Asia (SETA) research platform. His principal research interests are in environmental economics, institutional change, globalization, and sustainable development in Asia. He has published nearly 70 research papers in highly ranked journals including the American Journal of Agricultural Economics (A*), Journal of Development Studies (A), Ecological Economics (A*), Annals of Tourism Research (A*), Journal of Environmental Management (A), Asian Survey (A), Oxford Agrarian Studies, Journal of Hydrology (A*), Australian Journal of Agricultural and Resource Economics (A), and Australian Journal of Environmental Management. He has edited six books and the three most recent books are *Multi-criteria Decision Analysis in Environmental Management* with Professor Tony Prato, Missouri University, USA, *Child Labour in South Asia* with Associate Professor Kishor Sharma of Charles Sturt University, NSW Australia, and *Institutional Approach to Water Resources Management* published by Nova Publishers, New York. The first two books were published by Ashgate Publishing, UK. Besides, he had published 16 book chapters. Professor Gamini Herath has received close to RM 6 million in research grants in the past. He has refereed articles for many leading journals such as Ecological Economics, Ecological Modeling, Tourism Economics, Australian Journal of Environmental Management, Economic Record, Australian Journal of Agricultural and Resource Economics, and other recognized journals in environmental management. He has been a PhD examiner for La Trobe University, Charles Sturt University, Victoria University, Monash University, Sydney University, RMIT and

Griffith University, and the Asian Institute of Technology. Bangkok. He was a visiting professor at University of Montana, USA (1999), Missouri University USA (2004, 2008) and a visiting Scholar to the International Food Policy Research Institute, Washington DC (2002). Prior to joining Monash University Professor Gamini Herath worked at Deakin University and Las Trobe University Australia for nearly 17 years.

Index

www.ingramcontent.com/pod-product-compliance
Lightning Source LLC
Chambersburg PA
CBHW031325210326
41519CB00048B/3176